FITNESS WALKING

Scott Roberts, Ph.D.

TO:

AUNTIE LESLYN

LOVE

Scott 8/1/95

MASTERS PRESS

A Division of Howard W. Sams & Co.

Published by Masters Press
(A Division of Howard W. Sams & Co.)
2647 Waterfront Pkwy. E. Drive, Suite 300
Indianapolis, IN 46214

Roberts, Scott
        Fitness walking / Scott Roberts.
            p.   cm.
        ISBN 1-57028-034-7 (pbk.)
        1. Fitness walking. I. Title.
    RA781.65.R63   1995   95-299
    613.7'176--dc20   CIP

CONTENTS

ACKNOWLEDGEMENTS

Many people have helped me write this book. I would like to thank the following individuals for helping me create this book.

To Pam Brown for her photography expertise.

To Terry Farmer for modeling.

To Julia, Daniel and Andrew for helping out.

To the great staff at Master's Press.

To those individuals who taught me everything I know about exercise, including; Tom Fahey, Bill Colvin, Irv Faria, and Rob Robergs.

Cover design: Julie Biddle and Christy Pierce
Editor: Heather Seal
Production assistance: Terry Varvel, Phil Velikan, and Pat Brady

Dedication

The book is dedicated to my loving family.

My mom Patricia
My dad William
My sister Sharon
My brother Steven
My late sister Shelly
My wife Julia
And my sons Andrew, Daniel and Michael

April 1, 1995

CHAPTER 1

WALKING

The Sane Way to Achieving Lifelong Health and Fitness

Walking has become one of the most popular forms of aerobic exercise today. It has been estimated that over 77 million Americans walk on a "serious" basis. For proof, just take a look around your neighborhood in the morning or around office buildings at lunch time. What do you see? People out walking! It is interesting for me to think back when I was a competitive runner 8 years ago. When I was out running all I saw, or thought I saw, were people running. Today when I'm out walking as a confessed fitness walker, I mainly see people walking. Walking is being hailed as perhaps the safest and most effective form of aerobic exercise for anyone, young or old. Medical and fitness experts are routinely encouraging people to get out and walk as a way to improve their cardiovascular endurance, recover from an injury, prevent heart disease, lose weight, etc. Walking has truly come of age.

So why are so many more people out walking for exercise today than in the past? Besides the increased publicity of the benefits of exercise, one of the reasons is that it is so easy to do. Everyone, well, almost everyone, knows how to walk. We've been doing it all of our lives. It takes a while to master and enjoy jogging or cycling. Second, walking does not require any special equipment. All you need is a good pair of walking shoes. Third, walking can be performed anywhere. You don't need to join an expensive gym just to walk. You can walk outdoors or you can walk indoors; at a mall, for example. Research

1

Estimated Calories Burned Per Hour During Walking Versus Running				
Activity 100 lbs	120 lbs	150 lbs	180 lbs	200 lbs
Walking 204	258	318	372	426
Jogging 487	552	650	748	833

has shown that the easier and more convenient an exercise is to perform, the more likely an individual will stay with it. Fourth, most people enjoy getting out for a walk. What is better than taking a walk on a clear spring morning? And lastly, walking causes less injuries compared to other forms of aerobic exercise, such as jogging.

The Benefits of Walking for Fitness

Walking is a great way to improve your cardiovascular fitness level, tone upper body muscle groups and relieve stress. Walking is also a great way to lose weight. A recent study of obese women participating in either walking, stationary cycling or lap swimming, found that the women lost more body fat during walking than the other two exercises. The table above lists the average caloric cost of walking for different body weights.

Walking is a great way to get exercise without predisposing yourself to injury. During running, for example, each time the running foot hits the ground it produces forces approximately 150-200% of the runner's body weight, significantly more than during walking. Although the caloric cost of walking is relatively low when compared to jogging at slow speeds, when you walk briskly the caloric cost approaches that of jogging. Because walking is less intense than jogging or running, longer sessions can be maintained with less likelihood of injury.

The Benefits of Walking For Health

"Anyone contemplating an inactive lifestyle should have a thorough physical exam to see if his body can withstand it"

— P.O. Astrand

"Parts of the body unused and left idle become liable to disease, defective in growth and age quickly"

— Hippocrates

The benefits of regular physical activity and exercise have been the subject of provocative thoughts and intellectual curiosity for hundreds of years. Today, few individuals would debate the benefits of physical activity. Individuals who choose to be more physically active, in both their leisure and work activities, lower their risk for developing degenerative diseases such as osteoporosis, diabetes, obesity and cardiovascular disease.

The epidemiology (the study of disease patterns) of physical activity, morbidy and mortality has its origins in London, England. In the 1950s and 60s, Dr. Jeremy Morris began to look at the association between physical activity during work and the rate of cardiovascular disease. Dr. Morris began by comparing the rate and severity of cardiovascular disease between London bus conductors, who had to walk up and down the stairs and aisles of double decker buses collecting tickets, and the bus drivers who sat most of the day. Dr. Morris found that the conductors, who were more physically fit, had a lower incidence of coronary heart disease, a reduced fatality rate, and a lower rate of early mortality from the disease than the drivers. Based on Dr. Morris's early findings, he concluded that physical activity of work is a protection against ischaemic heart disease. Men in physically active jobs have less ischaemic heart disease during middle age, what disease they have is less severe, and they tend to develop it later than similar men in physically inactive jobs.

Since the studies of London bus conductors in the early 1950s, the epidemiology of leisure and occupational activity, health and disease has been investigated in hundreds of locations and occupations around the world. The consensus of the evidence from these studies is that physical activity has a protective effect against disease. More recently, Steven Blair studied the association between physical fitness and the risk of all-cause and cause-specific mortality in 10,224 men and 3,120 women. After an eight year follow-up, higher levels of physical fitness delayed all-cause mortality, primarily due to lowered rates of cardiovascular disease and cancer.

Exercise and Cardiovascular Disorders

"A man is only as old as his arteries."

— William Osler, M.D.

Cardiovascular disease continues to be the leading cause of death in the western world (American Heart Association, 1993). In 1990, diseases of the heart and blood vessels killed 930,000 Americans. From another perspective, more than two of every five Americans die of cardiovascular disease. The good news is that death rates from cardiovascular diseases have been on the decline. From 1980 to 1990, death rates from cardiovascular disease have declined 26.7 percent. The reduction in death rates for cardiovascular diseases can be linked to lifestyle changes among Americans and advances in medical treatments. Cardiovascular disease is still a major killer. But fortunately, cardiovascular disease is highly preventable.

Exercise plays an important role in preventing heart disease, as well as in the rehabilitation of individuals with heart disease. The major risk factors for coronary heart disease — hypertension, smoking, high cholesterol — are all positively affected by exercise. Furthermore, physical inactivity is now recognized as a major contributor to the atherosclerotic process. Walking is one of the safest and most effective ways to help prevent cardiovascular disease.

CHAPTER 2

GETTING STARTED

Exercise is generally quite safe for most people. The benefits of regular physical activity and exercise are becoming increasingly clear. Individuals who choose to be more physically active, in both their leisure and work activities, statistically lower their risk for developing degenerative diseases such as osteoporosis, diabetes, obesity and cardiovascular disease, to name a few. Despite the mounting evidence of the benefits of regular exercise, only 22% of adults engage in leisure time activities at or above the level recommended for health benefits in the U.S. Public Health Service's health and disease prevention goals and objectives for the nation.

The number of Americans who do not participate in regular exercise has been called an epidemic. Some of these sedentary individuals should be encouraged to learn that recent research has shown that you may not need to exercise as much as you thought to gain health-related benefits. The term "health-related fitness" now appears frequently in exercise literature to describe the health benefits of exercise. Instead of defining physical fitness in terms of one's athletic abilities (speed, power, balance, etc.), it is based on the five components of health-related physical fitness: cardiovascular fitness, muscular strength, muscular endurance, flexibility and body composition.

The simplest definition of health related physical fitness is the ability of the body's systems (heart, lungs, blood vessels, and muscles) to function efficiently, as to resist disease and to be able to participate in a variety of activities without undue fatigue. A comprehensive fitness program should have activities which develop and maintain each of the five components.

Summary of Selected Health Benefits Associated With Regular Exercise

Reduces the risk of cardiovascular disease
1. Increases HDL-cholesterol
2. Decreases LDL-cholesterol
3. Favorably changes the ratios between total cholesterol and HDL-C, and between LDL-C and HDL-cholesterol.
4. Decreases triglyceride levels
5. Promotes relaxation; relieves stress and tension
6. Decreases body fat and favorably changes body composition
7. Reduces blood pressure, especially if it is high
8. Makes blood platelets less sticky
9. Lessens cardiac arrhythmias
10. Increases myocardial efficiency
    a. Lowers resting heart rate
    b. Increases stroke volume
11. Increases oxygen-carrying capacity of the blood

Helps control diabetes
1. Makes cells less resistant to insulin
2. Reduces body fat

Promotes joint stability
1. Increases muscular strength
2. Increases strength in the ligaments, tendons, cartilage, and connective tissue.

Contributes to fewer low back problems

Acts as a stimulus for other lifestyle changes

Improves self-concept

Source: Anspaugh, D. J., Hamrick, M. H., & Rosato, F. D. Concepts and Applications of Wellness. P. 143, St. Louis, MO: Mosby-Year Book

Major Coronary Risk Factors

1. Diagnosed hypertension of systolic blood pressure > or = 160 or diastolic blood pressure > or = 90 mmHg on at least 2 separate occasions, or on antihypertensive medication.

2. Serum cholesterol > or = to 240 mg/dL.

3. Cigarette smoking

4. Diabetes mellitus

5. Family history of coronary or other atherosclerotic disease in parents or siblings before age 55.

The American College of Sports Medicine (ACSM) defines apparently healthy as individuals who are asymptomatic with no more than one of the major coronary risk factors listed above. Individuals who have symptoms suggestive of cardiac, pulmonary or metabolic disease, who have two or more coronary risk factors, or have known disease, should have a complete medical evaluation with a diagnostic exercise test prior to exercise. Safety should always be the primary factor dictating the readiness of an individual to exercise.

The American College of Sports Medicine, in conjunction with the Centers for Disease Control and Prevention (CDC) and the President's Council on Physical Fitness and Sports, recently issued a new recommendation on increased physical activity for Americans. The recommendation states that: "Every American adult should accumulate 30 minutes or more of moderate-intensity physical activity over the course of most days of the week. Because most Americans do not presently meet the standard described above, almost all should strive to increase their participation in moderate and/or vigorous physical activity."

The ACSM/CDC Position Statement on Exercise is perhaps the most powerful single event to have occurred in the last decade in the field of sports medicine and exercise physiology. The consensus statement means that a little bit of daily physical activity results in health-related benefits. Examples of activities that can contribute to the 30 minute total are: walking up stairs (instead of taking the elevator), gardening, raking leaves, walking at lunch. More typical forms of exercise — as running, swimming, cycling, working out at a health club, and playing tennis — are also encouraged. Individuals should strive to participate in activities that improve and maintain key components of health related fitness.

Components of Physical Fitness

The following is a summary of the five components of physical fitness.

Cardiovascular Fitness

Cardiovascular fitness is the most important component of physical fitness. Cardiovascular fitness is defined as the ability to perform moderate to high intensity exercise for long periods of time. During exercise, the body requires greater energy to perform the activity. Individuals with good cardiovascular fitness are able to deliver large amounts of oxygen to the working muscles without a significant amount of fatigue. Endurance trained individuals have a higher oxygen uptake (the ability to bring in and utilize oxygen) compared to sedentary individuals. One of the first things people notice after starting a walking program is that they have more energy. This is because the body is performing work at a lower energy cost. Cardiovascular fitness is improved by performing aerobic exercises such as walking, jogging, swimming, and cycling.

Muscular Strength

Muscular strength is defined as the maximal force or tension generated by a muscle or muscle group. Adequate muscular strength is important to everyone, both young and old. Strength is also important to good posture, personal appearance and self-image. From a health standpoint, strength helps burn fat and maintain weight, decrease the risk of injury and prevent chronic low back pain. Strength training is often an overlooked part of a fitness program. Muscular strength can be improved by lifting weights, performing calisthenic exercises or performing exercises using your own body weight.

Muscular Endurance

Muscular endurance is the ability of a muscle or group of muscles to contract repeatedly at a submaximal force or to sustain a submaximal force over a period of time. Muscular endurance is improved by performing exercises such as sit-ups and push-ups.

Flexibility

Flexibility is the range of motion possible in a joint or series of joints. Flexibility training is an important part of a balanced fitness program, but it is often overlooked. Flexibility training is often viewed as being unnecessary and time consuming. The potential benefits of stretching include: 1) increased performance, 2) increased joint stability, 3) increased joint range of motion, 4) enhanced warm-up results, 5) injury prevention, and 6) increased recovery time.

Body Composition

Body composition is the relative amount of muscle, bone and fat in the body. Excess weight is a serious medical, health and social issue. Since the evolution of industrialized societies, the incidence of obesity has risen dramatically. Aerobic exercise helps reduce body fat and increase lean body mass, both of which have a favorable impact on body composition. An ideal body fat percentage for good health is between 10 to 15% for young men and between 20 to 25% for young women. Body fat percentages greater than 20% for men or 30% for women are considered an indication of obesity.

General Principles of Exercise

An exercise program is based on eight key principles. These key principles include: 1) mode, 2) intensity, 3) frequency, 4) duration, 5) rate of progression, 6) the warm-up period, 7) the cool-down period and 8) the rest period. Each one of these components needs to be taken into consideration when developing an exercise program.

Warm-Up Period

The purpose of the warm-up period is to prepare the body for more vigorous activity and reduce the chance of injury. A gradual warm-up period increases the blood flow to the muscles, which actually warms the muscles so they can function effectively. The warm-up consist of a light aerobic period, followed by some flexibility exercises. The light aerobic period might consist of some light calisthenics, jogging in place, or 5 to 10 minutes on some stationary aerobic exercise equipment. The flexibility exercises described later in this chapter are appropriate during the warm-up period, but only after a brief aerobic exercise period. An adequate warm-up should last at least 10 minutes.

Cool-Down Period

The purpose of the cool-down period is to allow the body to gradually return to the resting state before exercise, or homeostasis. A gradual cool-down period or rhythmic exercise also facilitates return of blood to the heart, thus reducing the risk of venous pooling. The cool-down period basically consists of the same exercises as the warm-up period. The cool-down period should last between 10 and 15 minutes. The same types of activities and stretches can be performed during the cool-down period.

Mode

Mode refers to the type of activity performed during the exercise session. Various modes of exercise affect the components of fitness in different ways. For example, aerobic exercise affects aerobic capacity and body composition, but has little effect on muscular strength, flexibility and muscular endurance. Choosing the correct mode of exercise is important because it has a direct effect on the outcome. The mode of activities that improve cardiorespiratory endurance must use large muscle groups, rhythmically, for a continuous period of time (i.e. running, swimming, cycling, etc.). The mode of activities that develop muscular strength requires activities that work large and small muscle groups for brief periods of time (i.e. weight training).

Intensity

Intensity refers to the level of stress achieved during the exercise period. Exercise sessions can be low intensity or high intensity. Intensity is most often regulated by heart rate. However, other methods include breathing rate, an estimated percentage of maximal oxygen consumption or by rate of perceived exertion. In order to determine training heart rate, an individual's maximal heart rate must first be determined. An individual's maximal heart rate can be directly determined from a submaximal or maximal exercise test or it can be indirectly determined by subtracting one's age from 220. For example, an estimated maximal heart rate for a 20 year old is 200.

Low intensity exercise would be equal or 50-60% of an individual's maximum heart rate, whereas 85-90% would relate to high intensity exercise. When beginning an exercise program, it is best to start out at a low intensity and gradually increase the intensity over time. The training heart rate can either be taken as a direct percentage of the maximum heart rate obtained from an exercise test or it can be estimated from using a percentage of an individual's heart rate reserve.

	220
Age	-40
Maximal Heart Rate	180
Resting Heart Rate	-60
Heart Rate Reserve	120
Desired Intensity	x.60
	72
Resting Heart Rate	+60
Training Heart Rate	132

Another common method used to monitor exercise intensity is based on an individual's rate of perceived exertion (RPE). RPE is derived from the Borg Scale. A rating of 12 to 13 (using the 15-point scale) corresponds to approximately 60% of the heart rate range. Using the RPE scale is an easy and reliable way to monitor exercise intensity. The RPE scale is underutilized compared to heart rate when monitoring exercise intensity.

One of the simplest ways to monitor an individual's stress during exercise is the old "talk test." During light and comfortable exercise, you should be able to carry on a normal conversation with your exercise partner. If not, you are probably exercising at too high of an intensity.

BORG SCALE

6	
7	VERY, VERY LIGHT
8	
9	VERY LIGHT
10	
11	FAIRLY LIGHT
12	
13	SOMEWHAT HARD
14	
15	HARD
16	
17	VERY HARD
18	
19	VERY, VERY HARD
20	

Frequency

Frequency refers to the number of training sessions per week. It is recommended that individuals try to exercise 4 to 5 days per week. The frequency of exercise depends on: 1) the type of exercise performed, 2) the fitness status of the individual, and 3) the goals of the individual.

For sedentary individuals or individuals with a medical and/or health limitation, the frequency of exercise may be daily, since their ability to exercise at a high intensity or duration is limited. For sedentary individuals or individuals with a medical or health limitation, the frequency, duration and intensity of exercise may be significantly different compared to a healthy individual. For example, if an individual can only exercise for 5 to 10 minutes at a time, then they might have to exercise more frequently because they are not able to exercise for the recommended 30 to 40 minutes per session (4 to 5 days per week). Or they might have to exercise two times per day. Remember that frequency and duration are inversely related, meaning that if you exercise for a long period each session, then the frequency of your sessions will be reduced, and vice versa.

For apparently healthy individuals, greater frequency generally results in greater fitness benefits. However, exercise frequency needs to be carefully monitored and adjusted or injuries can result. The type of exercise performed also affects frequency. The components of fitness (flexibility, muscular strength and endurance, body composition and cardiorespiratory endurance) need to be equally balanced. Too much aerobic exercise often makes one too tired to lift weights, and vice versa.

Duration

Duration refers to the length of the training session. Duration and intensity are inversely related; that is, if the intensity of the exercise is high, the duration is generally low, and vice versa. Thirty to 40 minutes of continuous (aerobic) exercise is recommended per exercise session. In addition, time must be dedicated to flexibility and muscular training. The duration of the exercise session can be affected by environmental factors (heat, humidity, altitude, etc.). It can also be affected by the present fitness level of an individual and/or energy supply.

Rate of Progression

Rate of progression refers to how fast an individual progresses. Rate of progression is directly related to such factors as fatigue and drop out rate; that is, the faster the rate of progression, the greater the fatigue and probability of drop out. The intensity, duration and frequency should all be gradually increased over time (weeks to months, not days). The rate of progression can be affected by chronic injury or illness and will need to be modified if these problems persist. As individuals adapt to training, the rate of progression can be increased.

Rest

The amount of rest between workouts is just as important as the amount of time spent in workouts. Rest is needed between workouts to replace the energy stores in muscles (glycogen) and to let the overall body systems recover from training. If you push too hard, too long, your body will eventually break down. You should take at least one to two days per week.

Flexibility Training

Flexibility is defined as the range of motion in a given joint or combination of joints. Flexibility training is an important part of a balanced fitness program, but it is often overlooked even by experienced athletes. Flexibility training is often viewed as being unnecessary and time consuming. Although scientific evidence demonstrating the benefits of flexibility training is limited, it is generally agreed among most medical experts that flexibility training is important for optimal health and peak athletic performance.

Flexibility training is used in athletics to improve performance and reduce the possibility of injury, and in sports medicine fields as a component of injury treatment and rehabilitation. It is well known that a decrease in flexibility is inevitable with age and physical inactivity. One of the most common ailments for adults, chronic low-back pain, is primarily due to a decrease in flexibility, along with inadequate strength. Some sports require movement patterns that demand a great deal of flexibility, for example, the butterfly stroke in swimming. The importance of superior flexibility in sports such as basketball or football is debatable. Regardless, adequate flexibility should help to reduce muscle tension, improve posture and coordination, reduce body stiffness, possibly reduce injury and enhance exercise performance.

The potential benefits of stretching include: 1) increased performance, 2) increased joint stability, 3) increased joint range of motion, 4) enhanced warm-up results, 5) injury prevention and 6) increased recovery time. Numerous studies have reported improvements in joint mobility following flexibility training. An average improvement in joint mobility following flexibility training is approximately 5 to 20 percent. Other studies have looked at injury reduction as a result of stretching, with one such study reporting a 75% reduction in soccer injuries as a result of flexibility training. Another study using flexibility and strength training showed an improvement in 90% of patients with low back troubles. Other studies have reported a reduction in pain and accelerated injury rehabilitation as a result of stretching.

There are some potential risks associated with stretching. Attention has recently been focused on the timing of stretching. Current theory suggests that stretching be performed after a brief warm-up period. The logic behind such practice is based on the fact that preliminary movement raises the temperature of connective tissue, collagen becomes softer, and thus more elastic when heated. An increased potential for injury is possible if stretching is performed prior to an active warm-up. The risk of injury from stretching is greatest when performed by poorly conditioned individuals, individuals with a preexisting injury, and when stretches are performed with poor technique.

Static stretching is perhaps the safest and most effective form of stretching. Static stretching involves stretching the muscle and connective tissue of the joint passively to the extreme range of the joint. Static stretching exercises should be performed after a mild warm-up period in order to increase the temperature of the muscles and connective tissue. The static stretch should be held for about 8 to 12 seconds. During the performance of a static stretch, the position should always be held just below the threshold for pain. Static stretching causes gradual inhibition of the muscle spindle activation, which allows for greater long-term maintenance of range of motion (ROM).

Stretch #1

Heel Pull

Brace yourself against a solid object with one hand. With the opposite hand, grasp the top of your foot and slowly pull it toward your buttocks. Repeat with the opposite leg.

Stretch #2

Calf Stretch

Stand approximately 1-2 feet away from a wall or tree. Move one foot in close to the tree, while keeping the back leg straight behind you with the foot and heel flat on the ground. Slowly move your hips forward keeping your back foot on the ground. You should feel a slight stretch in your calf muscles. Repeat with the opposite leg.

Stretch #3

Hamstring Stretch

Rest one of your legs on an object 2-3 feet high. Keep the leg that is on the object straight and slowly bend forward. You should feel a slight stretch in your hamstring muscles. Repeat with the opposite leg.

Stretch #4

Shoulder Stretch

Grab one of your elbows with your opposite arm and pull it toward your body. Repeat with the opposite arm.

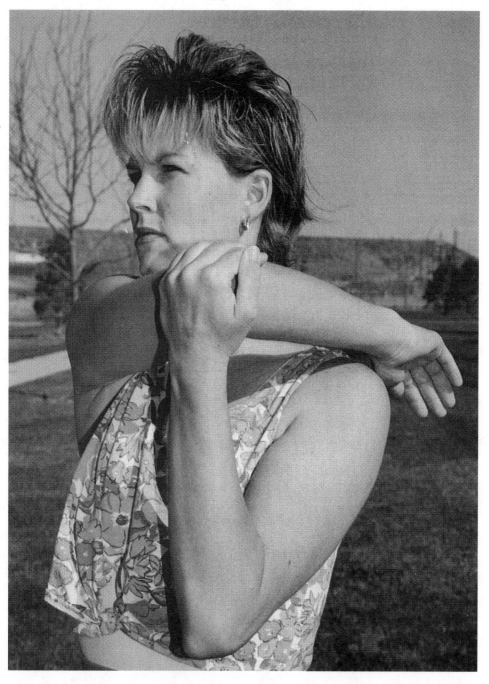

Stretch #5

Lunge

Place one of your feet about 12-18 inches in front of the other foot. Tuck your buttocks tightly under your hips while contracting your abdominal muscles. You should feel the stretch in the front of the hip region of the rear leg. Repeat with the other leg.

Cross Training

Cross training is a relatively new fitness term used to define fitness programs that have multiple modes. Athletes began cross training years ago in an effort to be able to sustain high volumes of training without getting injured or overtraining. An example of a cross training program might be walking on Monday, Wednesday and Friday, cycling on Tuesday and Thursday and resting on the weekend. For walkers, swimming and cycling are great substitutes for walking.

A Word On Overtraining

Overtraining occurs when your body is being pushed further than it is allowed to recover. Conditioning will actually decrease rather than increase thus exposing your body to injuries. Overtraining occurs when training plateaus or decreases over time. Usually overtraining is caused by poor program design, lack of adequate rest, and by not keeping a training log. It is important to plan training sessions so the intensity of the workouts increase gradually over time and you have adequate time to rest. Some warning signs of overtraining include:

1. Sleeplessness
2. Weight loss
3. Irritability
4. Problems in school or work
5. Loss of appetite
6. Increased injuries

Some preventative measures that can be taken are:

1. Get plenty of rest at night
2. Eat a well balanced diet
3. Vary your training schedule

We all know that exercise is important for good health, but it appears that few people do enough exercise to obtain any health related benefits. Walking is a great way to get sufficient exercise in order to get health related benefits. Remember to start slowly and progress slowly. Exercise has to be fun if you are going to stay with it.

CHAPTER 3

WALKING TECHNIQUE

Normal daily walking is an extremely easy task to perform. However, fitness walking does have some specific points that need to be followed to get the most benefit out of it. This chapter presents some essential information on good fitness walking technique. Once you practice it a few times, it will become second nature. As you become more and more comfortable with your walking technique, you will be able to walk faster, with less effort.

Upper Body Techniques

Technique #1 — Posture and Alignment

The upper body should be erect, with your chest up and out, shoulders relaxed, and abdominal muscles contracted with the rib cage lifted up. Good body alignment means that you are standing tall, yet keeping your posture relaxed, not tense. Imagine a midline running from the top of the head down through the middle of the body. Keep your body weight balanced and evenly distributed in relation to the imaginary midline.

Technique #2 — Arm Swing

Your arms should swing straight forward and remain as close to your body as possible. When you walk normally, your arms are straight downward. During fitness walking, your arms should be bent at a 90 degree angle at the elbow joint. When you are fitness walking, you want to pump your arms forward. Pumping your arms forward and backward helps you to walk faster, increase your energy expenditure and firm your muscles.

Lower Body Techniques

Technique #3 — Heel Contact

Walking consists of several movements or phases. First is the heel strike. As your lead leg swings forward, your heel should come in contact with the ground at about a 40 degree angle. Your lead leg should never come into contact with the ground flatfooted or on the ball of the foot.

Technique #4 — Heel-to-Toe Roll

Once your heel is planted with the lead leg, your body is propelled forward. You also begin to roll your foot forward. The natural roll should be from the back outside of the heel, through the midline of the foot to the toes. This phase of the walking stride is called the heel-to-toe

Technique #5 — Push-off

The last phase of the walking stride is the push-off. As you begin to walk faster, you will rely more on the push-off phase to propel you forward. As you increase your stride, your pace will increase. If you want, try to increase your walking stride, thrust your leading hip forward, and increase the pumping action of your arms.

Overall Techniques

Technique #6 — Economy of Movement

Runners and walkers try to be as economical as possible when exercising. This means that all of your movements should be performed so that you are propelled forward. An example of wasteful movements would be arms swinging out to the side excessively or feet kicking out to the side. When walking, think of yourself walking along an imaginary line. Try to place your feet one to two inches to the side of the imaginary line. Your feet, knees and arms should point straight forward.

Technique #7 — Breathing

Breathing is so natural, you wouldn't think you really need to concentrate on it during exercise, but you do. Breathing should follow a consistent rhythmic pattern throughout exercise. The intensity of your walking will determine the rate and depth of your breathing rate. Do not restrict inhalation to the nose. Inhale and exhale through the nose and mouth in a relaxed fashion. Never hold your breath during exercise.

Technique #8 — Hip Movement

As you become a more experienced walker, one of the things you are probably going to want to do is learn to walk faster. One easiest ways to learn to walk faster is to increase your stride length by turning your leading leg's hip forward. By turning your hips you allow your leading leg to move farther forward and your back leg back farther, versus up and down, thus improving your economy of movement.

Technique #9 — Leg Vault

Another technique used by experienced walkers to increase walking speed is to use your support leg as a vault to help you propel your body forward. Once your heel makes contact with the ground your whole leg becomes stiff (not locked at the knee) and your body pushes forward off of it as hard as possible.

Technique #10 — The Race Walk

The race walk is an advanced technique used by competitive race walkers. There are really only two rules that need to be followed in order to be race walking. The first rule (in competition) is the weight-bearing leg must be straight at the knee as the leg moves under the hip. The second rule is that one foot must have contact with the ground before the other foot leaves the ground.

One of the most unique aspects of race walking is hip movement. Hip movement during race walking is much different than during fitness walking. The unique hip action of race walkers increases their stride and force them forward. For more information on race walking, contact the American Racewalk Association, P.O. Box 18323, Boulder, Colorado, 80308-1323.

By following some simple tips, you can increase your walking speed and technique. Make sure you perfect your walking technique before you try to increase your pace. A faster walking pace will come with time.

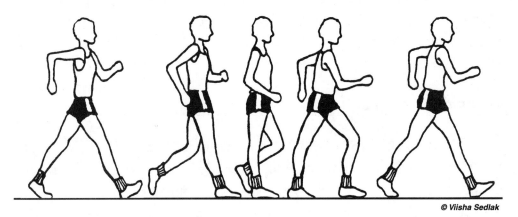

© Viisha Sedlak

The race walk

CHAPTER 4

ASSESSING YOUR READINESS TO BEGIN

Exercise is generally quite safe for most people. Problems do arise during or following exercise when people start an exercise program without knowing they have a medical or health condition that could be a worsened due to exercise. As people begin to increase their physical activity habits from a previously sedentary lifestyle, the risk of potential injury resulting from exercise increases. Before starting a walking program, it is important to determine whether or not you have any preexisting medical and/or health conditions that could affect the safety and effectiveness of your exercise program. The medical and health conditions listed in the table below may or may not be problematic to you, but only a physician can tell you for sure.

Common Health and Medical Problems That May Be Problematic To Exercise

Heart related problems
One or More Major Cardiac Risk Factor (see page 9)
Significant Emotional Distress (or other psychological problems)
Alcoholism or Other Drug Related Abuse Problems
Orthopedic Problems
A Recent Illness or Infection
Breathing Problems (asthma, etc.)
Extreme Sedentary Lifestyle

*Exercise may be appropriate for individuals with one or more of these conditions, if it is done so with the consent of a physician.

The purpose of this chapter is to assess your readiness to start a walking program. If, after you complete the pre-participation questionnaire below, you discover or suspect you have a medical or health related condition that may affect the safety and effectiveness of your walking program, you should consult with a physician before getting started. If for any reason you feel you may have a medical problem or condition that might affect your walking program, consult with a physician. Never take chances with your health. Also, if after you start your walking program you notice any unusual symptoms (muscle soreness or pain lasting several days, trouble breathing, pain or tightness in your chest, etc.) you should stop your walking program and consult with a physician right away.

Exercise Pre-Participation Health Quiz

The purpose of this quiz is to identify individuals who may need an exercise test or a more comprehensive medical evaluation before starting an exercise program.

1. Has a doctor ever said you have a heart condition and recommended only medically supervised physical activity?
2. Do you have chest pain bought on by physical activity?
3. Have you developed chest pain within the past month?
4. Do you tend to lose consciousness or fall over as a result of dizziness?
5. Do you have a bone or joint problem that could be aggravated by the proposed physical activity?
6. Has a doctor ever recommended medication for your blood pressure or a heart condition?
7. Are you aware, through your own experience or a doctor's advice, of any other physical reason against your exercising without medical supervision?

* If you answered yes to any one of the questions above, consult with a physician before starting a walking or exercise program.

How Is Your Health?

The American College of Sports Medicine recommends that men less than 40 years of age and women less than 50 years of age can start a moderate exercise program without a medical exam or exercise test if they are apparently healthy. Apparently healthy is defined as having no more than one major coronary risk factor (see page 9). If however, you have been sedentary for quite some time, it is advisable to consult with your physician before starting an exercise program. If you have two or more coronary risk factors, answered yes to any one of the questions in the pre-participation exercise quiz, or have any symptoms suggestive of a medical illness or problem, you should consult with a physician before starting an exercise program in order to ensure your program will be both safe and effective.

How Is Your Fitness ?

The Rockport Fitness Walking Test is a simple way to test your aerobic capacity. It was developed by medical and fitness experts as a way to assess cardiorespiratory endurance without expensive laboratory equipment. The only equipment needed to perform the test is a 440 yard track and a stop watch or a watch with a second hand. It is important to know what your aerobic capacity is in order to plan your walking and exercise program. If, after you finish the Rockport Fitness Walking Test, you fall into a low fitness category, it is advisable that you start off with a beginning walking workout program. If, however, you fall into a higher fitness category, you can start with an intermediate or advanced walking program. Another benefit of taking the Rockport Fitness Walking Test is that you can retest yourself later and see the improvement in your fitness level.

How To Take The Test

Before you take the Rockport Fitness Walking Test, complete the Physical Readiness Activity Quiz. If you feel there is any reason why you should not take the test, consult with your physician. If you don't have access to a track, find a flat, measured mile to walk on. Before you begin, take a few minutes to warm-up. You might want to do a warm-up session by walking a moderate pace for 1/4 to 1/2 mile. Some light stretching might also be beneficial (see chapter 2). The test is really quite simple. All you need to do is 1 mile as fast as you can walk (RUNNING IS NOT ALLOWED). If you start at a fast pace and begin to get fatigued or feel pain, just slow down. When you complete one mile, you need to record your time in minutes and seconds, and count your pulse rate for 15 seconds and record both figures.

How To Find Your Fitness Category

After you finish taking the Rockport Fitness Walking Test, look at pages 40 and 41 and find the appropriate table based on your sex and age group. Once you have your time and recovery heart rate, draw a vertical line through your time and a horizontal line through your heart rate (see example page 42). The point where the lines intersect is your fitness level.

Interpreting The Results

The Rockport Fitness Walking Test was designed to "estimate" your cardiorespiratory endurance, or aerobic capacity. It is not an exact measurement. The researchers who developed the test found that the test has an estimated error of less than 12 percent, compared to direct measurement of aerobic capacity in a laboratory setting. The charts are designed to tell you how fit you are compared to other individuals of your age and sex. The charts are based on weights of 170 pounds for men and 125 pounds for women. If you weigh substantially more, your relative cardiovascular fitness will be slightly overestimated, and vice versa if you weight substantially less.

Retesting

Every 6 months to 1 year, you should take the Rockport Fitness Walking Test to assess changes in your fitness level. As your fitness level improves, you will need to advance to more difficult walking programs if you want to continue to improve your aerobic capacity.

By now you should have a pretty good idea of whether or not you can start a walking program, or if you should see your physician first. If you think for any reason you should consult with your physician before getting started, do it! Don't be embarrassed to talk with your physician about getting started on an exercise program.

Relative Fitness Levels For The Rockport Fitness Walking Tests

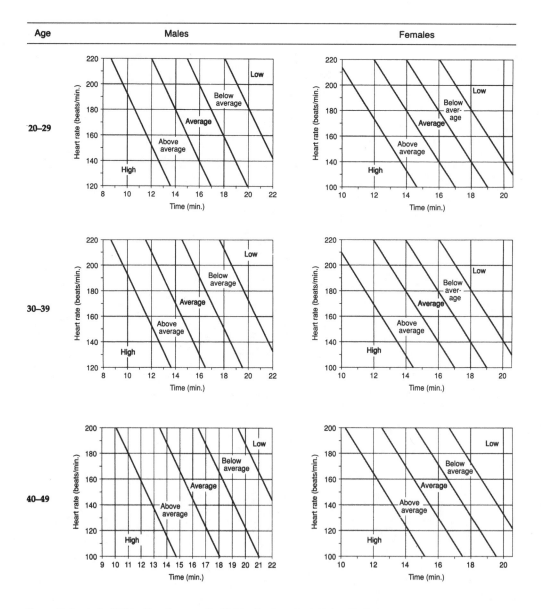

Age	Males	Females
	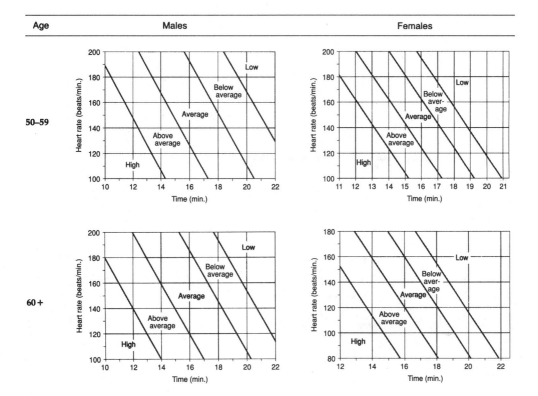	

Example of Completed Rockport Fitness Test Chart

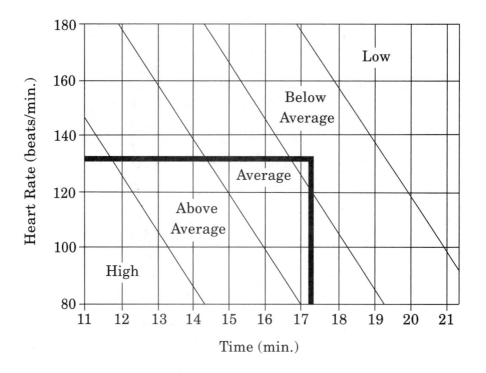

CHAPTER 5

EQUIPMENT

One of the best things about walking for exercise is that you need very little equipment to get started. This chapter gives some helpful tips on how to make your walking sessions safe and effective. In addition to the information contained in this chapter, you may also want to get advice from your physician, or podiatrist if you have one, on the best type of walking equipment for you. Today you will find most sporting goods salespeople very knowledgeable in their particular area of expertise. However, it is always a good idea to get information from several different sources. Another good source of information on equipment is in different walking and exercise magazines.

Shoes

Remember the days when you went to the sporting goods store to buy a pair of tennis shoes and you had only two choices to make, high or low top, and black or white? Boy, are those days gone forever. Today's sporting good stores have entire departments dedicated to shoes alone. There are men's, women's and children's shoes. There are separate sections for running, tennis, basketball, walking and cross training shoes. Even as a fitness expert with over 15 years experience in the fitness field, I get overwhelmed when I go to purchase a pair of shoes. I can only imagine what the average consumer must feel like.

Anatomy of Athletic Shoes

All shoes are not created equally. Today, athletic shoe companies have entire departments dedicated to research and development. In addition, there is a field of study called biomechanics that studies how the body reacts during a particular exercise so that the "ideal shoe" can be developed for that particular athletic activity. Can you imagine the difference in the performance of a world class marathon runner wearing a pair of high-top basketball shoes instead of light weight racing shoes! Or a golfer wearing a pair of sandals! Today, researchers take into account such factors as traction, friction and resiliency factors when designing a shoe. What will this person be doing when he/she is wearing these shoes?

The latest in walking shoes is based upon cushion mechanisms used in footwear designed for NASA. Many shoes today have midsoles that contract when the foot strikes the ground, generating a flow of energy through the length of the sole and terminating in a potential upward force. The shoes actually act as a spring. One of the greatest innovations in the athletic shoe was invented by a track coach in Eugene, Oregon. Bill Boweran filled a waffle toasting iron with urethane, producing an outer-sole that resembled a waffle. This shoe revolutionized the athletic apparel industry, as the "waffle" design running shoe was the birth of the Nike Corporation.

Any shoe has several basic components; the outer sole, the mid-sole, the inner sole and the outer upper sole. The outer sole is the material on the bottom of the shoe that comes in contact with the ground. Today, outer soles are made from a variety of materials, all designed to provide stability and resiliency. If you compare a running shoe and a walking shoe, you will notice some distinct differences. A running shoe has a thicker heel and may have a rougher looking bottom for better traction. For running, shock absorption is a must. When walking, you don't need as much shock absorption, thus the difference in thickness. It is important to look at the pattern of wear on the bottom of the sole. Excessive wear on the outside or inside of the shoe may indicate the need for special shoes or special devices called orthotics that correct for anatomical abnormalities.

The mid-sole is the heart and soul of the shoe. The primary purpose of the mid-sole is to provide shock absorption. Early mid-soles were made out of rubber, which added to the weight of the shoe. In the late 70s, a material called ethylene vinyl acetate (EVA) was invented which made a better shock absorber with less weight. The only disadvantage with EVA is that with time, the EVA compresses down, decreasing the shock absorption of the shoe. When the mid-sole gets harder, or you notice your feet or legs hurting more, you probably need new shoes. People get confused about when to get a new pair of shoes, because the mid-sole may wear out before the bottom sole. Just because you still have good tread on the bottom-sole, you may still need to replace your shoes because the mid-sole has worn out.

The inner sole is what comes in direct contact with your feet. Most inner soles have removable inner inserts. These inner soles can be replaced with commercially available replacements when the original ones wear out. In addition, if you need to wear orthotics, you man need to remove the original inner soles or modify them for the orthotics. Another characteristic of the inner part of the shoe is the heel portion. Good shoes have a hard heel support. The purpose of the heel support is to help stabilize the foot during exercise.

The upper outer part of shoe varies greatly between shoes and different manufacturing companies. Many shoe companies spend more money on outer appearance than inner quality, so don't be fooled by fancy appearances (lights, colors, etc.). The upper part of the shoe can be made of leather, nylon or a combination of the two. Nylon is easier to clean and allows for good circulation, whereas leather is preferable in cold weather.

Qualities Of A Good Walking Shoe

Comfortable
Affordable
Flexible
Provide adequate shock absorption
Preferably designed as a walking shoe
Easy to clean
Provide good support

Clothing

Choosing the right clothing will allow you to enjoy winter and summer exercise, despite extreme temperatures. Clothing provides protection from the elements by increasing the insulating capacity of the body. It is best to dress in layers, so that clothing can be removed in an effort to rid the body of excess body heat. Don't be forced to go from one extreme to another.

Layering should start with a good set of synthetic long underwear, such as those made out of polypropylene. Polypropylene actually draws perspiration away from the skin so that evaporative cooling does not increase heat loss from the body. The next layer should be one or two long shirts or a sweater, followed by a waterproof wind-breaker or jacket. It is important to remember that the insulating quality of clothing is dramatically reduced once it gets wet. Better quality winter clothing (i.e., Gortex™) provides insulation and still allows loss of water vapor.

Summer clothing should allow for maximum evaporation. Shorts and T-shirts are preferable. Remember, though, that maximum evaporation comes at a cost. By increasing your skin exposure, you are also increasing your exposure to the sun. Always remember to use sun block if you plan on being out in the sun for an extended period of time.

Good quality cotton socks are a must. Cotton socks help absorb sweat, while protecting your feet from your shoes. Shorts should be comfortable, that's about it. Some people prefer to wear running shorts or athletic shorts, but they are not necessary. Women should wear an athletic bra for maximum support. In the summer tank tops and halter tops are fine, just remember to use sunblock. Remember that winter clothing should consist of light layers. Try to avoid wearing heavy coats during walking, as they do not allow for good ventilation.

Other Equipment

Using hand weights during walking increases your heart rate and energy expenditure, while at the same time toning your muscles. You should gradually get used to using hand weights during exercise. Don't start out carrying 5 pound dumbbells for your normal 5 mile walk without first taking time to get used to small weights at shorter distances. Using hand weights will alter your normal arm swing pattern and will add stress to your elbows and shoulders. The risk of injury, as well as the benefits from using handweights during walking are minimal. Individuals with high blood pressure or cardiovascular disease should avoid using hand weights during aerobic exercise. The use of ankle weights during walking is not advised as they tend to alter your normal walking gate, and can lead to injuries.

Other equipment important to walkers is shown in the picture below. Sunglasses are important to help protect your eyes from direct and reflective sun rays. Women may feel comfortable carrying mace or some other type of security device. A fanny pack can hold lots of things, such as water, spare change, a cellular phone, etc. When walking at night, it is important to wear reflective clothing or a reflective vest. Wearing a hat helps protect your face, neck and ears from direct sunlight. If you are planning on a long walk, it is important that you carry water with you. Several companies make waist belts that hold water bottles.

Walking, compared to many other types of exercise and sports is unique in that it does not require a great deal of expensive equipment in order to get started. The only real major investment is a good pair of shoes. Other than that, most of the other equipment can probably be found in your closet or dresser.

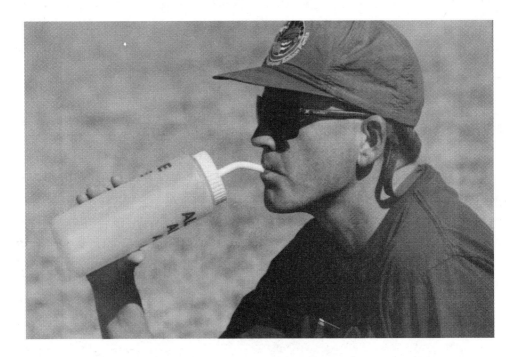

CHAPTER 6

SAFETY

Exercise is generally quite safe. There are some factors that increase the chances of injury during exercise. These factors include exercising in extreme environmental conditions, exercising in the night, exercising around cars or dogs and exercising too much. This chapter presents some common sense tips to help your walking program be as safe as possible.

Exercising In The Heat

As summer approaches, even the most dedicated fitness enthusiasts start thinking of ways to avoid exercising in the heat. Understandably, exercising during the peak days of summer is not an enjoyable experience. While summer may not be the most popular time to exercise, following some basic guidelines and training considerations will remarkably improve heat tolerance and performance level when exercising in the heat.

For most individuals performing physical activity in the heat requires a great deal of effort, and the performance is generally less than ideal. Overexposure to heat while exercising not only results in decreased work performance, but also a predisposition to serious heat illness. By adequately preparing for the summer months, athletes can avoid most of the discomforts associated with exercising in the heat, and prevent serious heat illness.

Heat Training Considerations

Human beings are able to live, work and exercise relatively independent of the environment because of their ability to maintain constant body temperatures. Humans are homeotherms, which means that their internal temperatures must be regulated. A large variance from the normal resting body temperature of 98.6° Fahrenheit can be catastrophic. Heat must be removed from the body or body temperature will climb and cause disastrous overheating.

The most important function of sweating is to cool the body. Cooling only takes place when sweat evaporates from the skin. It is important to note that evaporation is greatly affected by the relative humidity. Relative humidity is the amount of water vapor in the air, relative to the amount it can hold. As the relative humidity increases, heat loss through evaporation decreases. Special precautions should be taken when sweat drips off the body during or following exercise. It probably means that the temperature is low, but the humidity is high, and evaporative cooling is not taking place. It may not be possible to regulate temperature when exercising on a hot, humid day. It is under such conditions that most heat illness occurs.

Four environmental factors determine the ability to lose heat, they are: 1) wind speed, 2) humidity, 3) the temperature of the air and 4) the amount of radiant heat. Loss of heat is increased by circulating air. Exercising in cool wind or during a slight breeze will help facilitate cooling. Heat is also lost through radiation when the body temperature is warmer than the surrounding environment. Thus, running in the shade is better than running in the direct sun light. If possible, exercise sessions should take place during the coolest period of the day. Use caution when exercising on hot, dry, windless days, or on days when the humidity is high.

The best way to avoid serious heat injuries is to prepare in advance for changing environmental conditions. Allowing the body to gradually acclimatize to the heat will make exercising in it more comfortable and tolerable. Acclimatization improves the circulatory

Guidelines For Exercising In The Heat

1. Splash water on the skin.

2. Plan for regular water breaks during an exercise session.

3. Schedule exercise sessions during the cooler times of the day.

4. Avoid the use of salt tablets.

5. Drink plenty of water prior to exercising in the heat.

6. Avoid high intensity training on days with no cloud cover and high humidity.

7. Drink a fluid that is cold (8 to 13°C), low in sugar (<2.5 g/dl), with little or no electrolytes.

8. Be well conditioned prior to exercising in the heat.

and sweating responses, which facilitate heat dissipation. Acclimatization is accomplished by a progressive exercise program performed in the heat for 1 to 2 weeks, not by merely sitting around in the sun. Improved heat tolerance is associated with an early onset of sweating and increased sweat production. Another important benefit of acclimatization is a lowered skin temperature during exercise. A lower skin temperature in the heat means that less blood flow is required to transfer excess heat; thus, exercise performance is enhanced.

Thermal Distress

Anyone who exercises in the heat should be familiar with four reactions resulting from overexposure to the heat. It is important to note that heat illness can be prevented through proper conditioning, gradual acclimatization, and adequate fluid replacement. Athletes need to think ahead, and plan for special precautions when exercising in the heat.

In an attempt to counterbalance overheating, the human body increases sweat rates. Sweat is over 99% water; thus, prolonged profuse sweating may cause dehydration. Water deficits totalling 6-10% of selected athletes' body weights have been reported. Dehydration in the excess of 5% of total body weight severely limits sweating and circulatory capacity, and exposes athletes to severe health hazards. The best prevention against dehydration is adequate fluid replacement before, during and after exercise. It is important to note that fluid requirements usually never keep pace with body requirements and sweat losses. As long as water consumption equals sweat loss, dehydration can be prevented. Athletes who train frequently in the heat should keep a record of their weight. An athlete who loses 2 to 3% of his total body weight after a workout should not exercise again until adequate rehydration takes place.

Heat cramps are characterized by painful spasms of the muscles following hard work in the heat, usually caused by inadequate fluid replacement. The most common treatment for heat cramps is to move to a cool environment and drink cold liquids. Drinking plenty of fluids prior to, during and after exercise should help prevent heat cramps.

Heat exhaustion is a condition brought on by overexposure to the heat. It is characterized by weakness, dizziness, nausea, profuse sweating, headaches and eventually collapse. Treatment for heat exhaustion includes having the subject lie down in a shaded area and administering fluids. Emergency medical attention may be needed if the subject's condition does not improve.

Heat stroke is a life-threatening reaction to heat exposure. It is characterized by a high body temperature, usually above 105-106 Fahrenheit, cessation of sweating, rapid pulse and respiratory rate and usually elevated blood pressure. Anyone suspected of suffering from heat stroke should be taken to emergency facilities immediately.

Exercising In The Cold

How are humans able to exercise in extremely cold environments without freezing to death? For two reasons: first, because we are intelligent enough to dress warmly and get out of the cold when we need to, and second, because of our ability to regulate body temperature. Body temperature is regulated by means of receptors in the skin and muscles that are sensitive to changes in the ambient temperature, as well as by means of a master regulating center in the brain that senses changes in the temperature of the blood. During exposure to cold weather, these mechanisms work together to increase heat production in a effort to maintain body temperature.

The most immediate threat from exposure to the cold is the influence of wind on the body's surface. Wind increases the rate of cold air molecules coming in contact with the skin so that heat loss is accelerated. When the temperature drops from 20°F to 0°F and the wind speed picks up from 5-15 mph, because of the windchill factor the temperature feels like -36°F.

Below is a windchill index chart that outlines the interaction between temperature and wind speed. Use the chart as a guide to plan winter exercise sessions. If possible, begin exercising against the wind, and return with the wind to your back. Use extreme caution in exercising when the windchill index is in the Increasing Danger zone, and try to avoid exercise altogether if the index is in the Great Danger zone.

Wind Chill Factor Chart

ESTIMATED WIND SPEED (mph)	ACTUAL THERMOMETER READING (°F)											
	50	40	30	20	10	0	-10	-20	-30	-40	-50	-60
	EQUIVALENT TEMPERATURE (°F)											
Calm	50	40	30	20	10	0	-10	-20	-30	-40	-50	-60
5	48	37	27	16	6	-5	-15	-26	-36	-47	-57	-68
10	40	28	16	4	-9	-24	-33	-46	-58	-70	-83	-95
15	36	22	9	-5	-18	-32	-45	-58	-72	-85	-99	-112
20	32	18	4	-10	-25	-39	-53	-67	-82	-96	-110	-124
25	30	16	0	-15	-29	-44	-59	-74	-88	-104	-118	-133
30	28	13	-2	-18	-33	-48	-63	-79	-94	-109	-125	-140
35	27	11	-4	-20	-35	-51	-67	-82	-98	-113	-129	-145
40	26	10	-6	-21	-37	-53	-69	-85	-100	-116	-132	-148

	Green	Yellow	Red
Wind speeds greater than 40 mph have little additional effect.	LITTLE DANGER (for properly clothed person). Maximum danger of false sense of security.	INCREASING DANGER Danger from freezing or exposed flesh.	GREAT DANGER

Source: National Weather Service

Guidelines For Exercising In The Cold

1. Take time to plan ahead before exercising in cold weather.

2. Make use of the many technological advances in winter clothing. Although high-tech clothing may cost more, it will allow you to have a safer and more enjoyable experience. Also remember to dress in layers.

3. Wear a scarf or winter mask over your mouth to lessen the sensation of the cold air.

4. Even though it is cold out, you still need to drink lots of cold fluids to prevent dehydration.

5. Be careful of your fatigue level. Fatigue is the fastest way to develop a case of hypothermia.

6. Try to avoid facing the wind when exercising in the cold. If there is no alternative, protect as much of your exposed flesh as possible.

7. Watch for changes in the weather. Always be thinking ahead.

Cold Weather Injuries

Exposure to the cold and wind increases the risk of cold weather injuries. The two most common cold weather injuries are frostbite and hypothermia. Frostbite is a term used to refer to skin that has been damaged from exposure to extreme cold or windchill. Frostbite usually occurs when skin temperature falls below -20°F. Exercising when the ambient temperature is above 20°F poses little danger of exposure to frostbite.

Breathing Cold Air During Exercise

A persistent myth regarding exercising in the cold is that lungs can freeze when exposed to cold air for a long period of time. In fact, the human pulmonary system is extremely efficient at adapting to changing environmental conditions. The nose, mouth and trachea add water vapor to inhaled air, warm and/or cool it to body temperature, and trap any foreign matter (e.g., dust, yeast, and bacteria) as well as chemical pollutants in the air. Because inhaled air is significantly warmed before it reaches the delicate smaller bronchi and other lung tissue, the danger of lung tissue freezing is very remote. To lessen the irritation of breathing in cold air, try wearing one of the more sophisticated cold weather face masks or a scarf over your mouth.

Walking Smart

Walking smart means thinking and looking ahead. Unfortunately, there are individuals who want to harm people, even people that exercise. Consider carrying mace or another type of protection device. Look out for areas or situations that do not look safe (i.e. walking through an alley for a short cut). I know some walkers who carry a cellular phone with them. Always remember that safety is increased with numbers, meaning that it is best to exercise with someone else if you can. If you are traveling, ask the hotel staff where the safest area to exercise is. When traveling, sometimes it is a better idea to exercise in the hotel gym or go to a shopping center to walk. Report to the police any unusual or illegal situations that happen to you. Always try to be a "safe walker."

Cars

It is always advisable to walk in an area where there is not much car traffic. Sidewalks are preferable over roads. If you have to walk on the road, always face traffic. When you approach an intersection, take time to look out for traffic. Wearing headphones is not advisable if you are walking in a high traffic area.

Dogs

Dogs may be man's best friend, but they are often not walkers' best friends. When you are walking, you always need to think and look ahead. I generally carry some small stones with me just in case. If a dog approaches you, stop and wait to see what its intentions are. Most times dogs are friendly and will just keep going. If a dog approaches and growls, try yelling or stomping your feet to scare them. Yelling will also draw the attention of the dog's owner if he is home. As a last resort, try throwing something toward the dog without hurting him. You may also have to jump up on to something or jump over a fence to avoid a vicious dog. Always report dog attacks. On the next page are pictures that demonstrate how to handle a dog encounter.

Night Walking

Walking at night poses several problems. First and foremost, visibility is decreased at night. Second, the safety factor is decreased. It is more difficult for you to see where you are going and it is harder for other people to see you as well. If you have to walk at night, try to walk in a well lit area. In addition wear a reflective vest to help people see you. You may also want to carry a flashlight with you as well. It is generally less safe to walk at night than in the daytime.

CHAPTER 7

WALKING FOR FITNESS

Before you begin your walking program, make sure you have read the preceeding chapters. By now you should know the following: a) whether or not you are ready to begin an exercise program (i.e., do not have any medical and/or health limitations that would make exercise inadvisable), b) how to monitor your exercise intensity, c) how to warm-up and cool-down, including stretching exercises, d) what equipment you will need, and e) the basic techniques involved in fitness walking. Now it is time to get started with your walking program. Remember that when you are walking for fitness, almost any distance and any pace will help improve your fitness level. It is also important to realize that the more sedentary you currently are, the greater will be your initial improvement in fitness.

Listed at the end of this chapter are 3 different walking programs. Which one you choose to start with depends on your current fitness level and health status. If you are currently sedentary, fall into the low to below average fitness category after completing the walking fitness test, or have known medical and/or health limitations, you should start with the beginning walking program. If you are currently somewhat active, fall into the average to above average fitness category, and do not have or have only limited medical and/or health limitations, you can start with the intermediate program. If you are currently quite active, fall into the high fitness category, and do not have any medical and/or health limitations, you can start with the advanced program.

The three different programs outlined below are based on differences in time spent in the exercise training mode. As you get in better shape, you will need to exercise for longer periods of time, and possibly at higher intensity levels, in order to continue to make improvements in your fitness level. In addition to the duration of your walking sessions, it is also important to consider the FREQUENCY, INTENSITY and PROGRESSION RATE of your exercise as well. Generally speaking, if you have been sedentary for awhile it would be advisable to start with the beginning program of frequency, intensity and progression rate (i.e. 3 to 4 days per week, 55 to 65% of your maximum heart rate and progress in exercise time at a rate of 3 to 5% per week).

What happens when you finish one of the 12 week programs? You can do several things. First, you can stay where you are and not make any changes at all. Once you have reached a certain point in your fitness level and are comfortable with your results, you can move into a maintenance phase. That means that you are doing just enough exercise to maintain your fitness level — you are not interested in improving it any more. Second, you can increase the exercise duration by continuing to add on additional exercise time every week until you get to a point where you are satisfied. Third, you can increase the exercise time (or keep it the same) but increase the exercise training intensity. Fourth, you can increase the frequency of your exercise training. What changes you make are dependent on how well you feel after finishing one of the 12 week programs, and what your fitness goals are.

Example

Bob is a sedentary 45-year-old male who wants to begin a walking program. His maximum heart rate (MHR) is 175. According to the walking test he falls into the average fitness category. He has no real medical and/or health limitations except for a chronic low back problem. Because of his young age and average level of fitness, Bob decided to begin with the intermediate walking program. Thus, Bob's training program is based on 4 to 5 days per week of walking, at a training heart rate of 114 to 131 beats per minute. Bob did fine and completed the 12 week intermediate program with no problems. He did, however, feel that he still wanted to make more improvement in his fitness level so he decided to exercise 5 to 6 days per week, for 40 to 50 minutes per session at a higher exercise intensity level. Bob did fine for several weeks with the changes, but soon felt more stress in his lower back than normal and more overall fatigue. When he went back to his 4 to 5 days per week, regular exercise intensity and duration level, his back problems went away, and his fitness continued to improve.

So what can we learn from Bob's experiences? First, that he started out conservatively. He did not experience any problems during the first 12 weeks because he followed the program carefully, making sure he stayed within his training heart rate zone and slowly progressed each week. But when he finished, he decided to add more days, more time and exercise at a higher exercise intensity. When he changed three different components of his exercise program, he began to experience excessive fatigue and more discomfort in his back. When he went back to his old routine, his back pain and fatigue went away. The lesson to learn is NEVER MAKE HASTY AND EXCESSIVE CHANGES IN YOUR EXERCISE PROGRAM.

Before you start your walking program, you should remember three important points: 1) you need to be patient (improvement in your fitness level will not happen overnight), 2) improvements in your fitness level come in small increments (the most rapid improvements happen in the first months), and 3) you should always make small and infrequent increases in your program. If you follow these simple guidelines you will enjoy your walking program and the benefits that come along with it as well.

Other Training Considerations

FREQUENCY

3 TO 4 DAYS/WEEK	BEGINNING
4 TO 5 DAYS/WEEK	INTERMEDIATE
5 TO 6 DAYS/WEEK	ADVANCED

INTENSITY

55 TO 65% OF MHR	BEGINNING
65 TO 75% OF MHR	INTERMEDIATE
75 TO 85% OF MHR	ADVANCED

PROGRESSION

5 to 7%	TIME/WEEK	BEGINNING
7 to 9%	TIME/WEEK	INTERMEDIATE
9 to 11%	TIME/WEEK	ADVANCED

Beginning Program

week	warm-up walk	training pace	cool-down walk	total exercise time
WEEK 1	5 MIN.	7 MIN.	5 MIN.	17 MIN.
WEEK 2	5 MIN.	9 MIN.	5 MIN.	19 MIN.
WEEK 3	5 MIN.	11 MIN.	5 MIN.	21 MIN.
WEEK 4	5 MIN.	13 MIN.	5 MIN.	23 MIN.
WEEK 5	5 MIN.	15 MIN.	5 MIN.	25 MIN.
WEEK 6	5 MIN.	18 MIN.	5 MIN.	28 MIN.
WEEK 7	5 MIN.	20 MIN.	5 MIN.	30 MIN.
WEEK 8	5 MIN.	23 MIN.	5 MIN.	33 MIN.
WEEK 9	5 MIN.	26 MIN.	5 MIN.	36 MIN.
WEEK 10	5 MIN.	28 MIN.	5 MIN.	38 MIN.
WEEK 11	5 MIN.	30 MIN.	5 MIN.	40 MIN.
WEEK 12	5 MIN.	32 MIN.	5 MIN.	42 MIN.

Intermediate Program

week	warm-up walk	training pace	cool-down walk	total exercise time
WEEK 1	5-7 MIN.	8 MIN.	5-7MIN.	18-22 MIN.
WEEK 2	5-7 MIN.	10 MIN.	5-7 MIN.	20-24 MIN.
WEEK 3	5-7 MIN.	12 MIN.	5-7 MIN.	22-26 MIN.
WEEK 4	5-7 MIN.	14 MIN.	5-7 MIN.	24-28 MIN.
WEEK 5	5-7 MIN.	16 MIN.	5-7 MIN.	26-30 MIN.
WEEK 6	5-7 MIN.	19 MIN.	5-7 MIN.	29-33 MIN.
WEEK 7	5-7 MIN.	21 MIN.	5-7 MIN.	31-35 MIN.
WEEK 8	5-7 MIN.	24 MIN.	5-7 MIN.	34-38 MIN.
WEEK 9	5-7 MIN.	27 MIN.	5-7 MIN.	37-41 MIN.
WEEK 10	5-7 MIN.	29 MIN.	5-7 MIN.	39-43 MIN.
WEEK 11	5-7 MIN.	31 MIN.	5-7 MIN.	41-45 MIN.
WEEK 12	5-7 MIN.	33 MIN.	5-7 MIN.	43-47 MIN.

Advanced Program

week	warm-up walk	training pace	cool-down walk	total exercise time
WEEK 1	5-10 MIN.	12 MIN.	5-10 MIN.	22-32 MIN.
WEEK 2	5-10 MIN.	14 MIN.	5-10 MIN.	24-34 MIN.
WEEK 3	5-10 MIN.	16 MIN.	5-10 MIN.	26-36 MIN.
WEEK 4	5-10 MIN.	18 MIN.	5-10 MIN.	28-38 MIN.
WEEK 5	5-10 MIN.	20 MIN.	5-10 MIN.	30-40 MIN.
WEEK 6	5-10 MIN.	23 MIN.	5-10 MIN.	33-43 MIN.
WEEK 7	5-10 MIN.	25 MIN.	5-10 MIN.	35-45 MIN.
WEEK 8	5-10 MIN.	29 MIN.	5-10 MIN.	39-49 MIN.
WEEK 9	5-10 MIN.	32 MIN.	5-10 MIN.	42-52 MIN.
WEEK 10	5-10 MIN.	33 MIN.	5-10 MIN.	43-53 MIN.
WEEK 11	5-10 MIN.	35 MIN.	5-7 MIN.	45-55 MIN.
WEEK 12	5-10 MIN.	40 MIN.	5-7 MIN.	55-60 MIN.

CHAPTER 8

EXERCISE AND GOOD NUTRITION

Most Americans are obsessed with weight. In fact, on any given day, at least one out of every four Americans is on a diet. Americans spend over 30 billion dollars annually on various weight loss methods, most of which fail. Americans are constantly being told that they should or shouldn't eat a particular food — it's too fat, it's got too many additives in it! From a public health standpoint, the obsession with nutrition and excess body weight is probably good. Excess body weight is associated with numerous health-related problems, including increased risk for coronary artery disease, diabetes and hyperlipidemia. Unfortunately, the majority of dieters are unsuccessful at keeping the weight off after dieting. In addition, an obsession with weight and weight loss can lead to practices of self-imposed starvation (anorexia nervosa) which is a serious medical problem. The importance of maintaining a healthy body weight and eating nutritiously is important, but not an easy task for most people.

The problems associated with excess weight, weight loss and weight control are multifaceted. How to lose and maintain weight is difficult for most people to understand. Sure, everybody's been told that if you want to lose weight, just stop eating so much and get more exercise. If it sounds so simple, why are so many Americans overweight, and why do so many people fail at losing weight? Because most people simply do not understand the complexity of weight loss and weight maintenance.

Excess Weight

Excess weight is a serious medical and social issue. Since the evolution of industrialized societies, the incidence of obesity has risen dramatically. There is no longer a need to hunt or pick one's food; we just drive by a window or go to a super market. The ease of obtaining food, combined with the fact that most people today work in sedentary professions, has led to an epidemic of obesity in the United States and in other nations as well. Today it takes a conscious effort to increase your physical activity level and choose foods that are good for you. Even most well-educated people do not feel they have the time or knowledge to eat healthy and get enough exercise.

1983 Metropolitan Life Insurance Height and Weight Table

Height	Small Frame	Medium Frame	Large Frame
		Weight in pounds	
Men*			
5'2"	128-134	131-141	138-150
5'3"	130-136	133-143	140-153
5'4"	132-138	135-145	142-156
5'5"	134-140	137-148	144-160
5'6"	136-142	139-151	146-164
5'7"	138-145	142-154	149-168
5'8"	140-148	145-157	152-172
5'9"	142-151	148-160	155-176
5'10"	144-154	151-163	158-180
5'11"	146-157	154-166	161-184
6'0"	149-160	157-170	164-188
6'1"	152-164	160-174	168-192
6'2"	155-168	164-178	172-197
6'3"	158-172	167-182	176-202
6'4"	162-176	171-187	181-207
Women†			
4'10"	102-111	109-121	118-131
4'11"	103-113	111-123	120-134
5'0"	104-115	113-126	122-137
5'1"	106-118	115-129	125-140
5'2"	108-121	118-132	128-143
5'3"	111-124	121-135	131-147
5'4"	114-127	124-138	134-151
5'5"	117-130	127-141	137-155
5'6"	120-133	130-144	140-159
5'7"	123-136	133-147	143-163
5'8"	126-139	136-150	146-167
5'9"	129-142	139-153	149-170
5'10"	132-145	142-156	152-173
5'11"	135-148	145-159	155-176
6'0"	138-151	148-162	158-179

*Weights at ages 25 to 59, based on lowest mortality. Weight in pounds according to frame (in indoor clothing weighing 5 lb, shoes with 1" heels).
†Weights at ages 25 to 59, based on lowest mortality. Weight in pounds according to frame (in indoor clothing weighing 3 lb, shoes with 1" heels).

Source: Hahn/Payne. Focus On Health, 1994 — Mosby-Year Book, Inc.

How Fat Are You ?

Weight tables, although convenient, are limited in their ability to provide accurate estimates of ideal weight for the entire population. Your waist divided by your hip (waist-to-hip-ratio) provides another measure of weight status. A waist-to-hip ratio greater than 1.0 is an indication of being overweight. Remember the pinch test .... "if you can pinch more than an inch, you're fat" There may be some validity to this test, although crude. This test is theoretically the same test used when performing skinfold measurements. A good sign that you're losing body weight, and probably fat, is when you find yourself having to adjust your belt tighter. Of course the reverse is true as well when you are gaining weight!

Defining Obesity and Overweight

Two terms are often used to classify excess weight: overweight and obese. Obese literally means "excess fat." Obesity refers to excess body fat, versus body weight. An ideal body fat percentage for good health is between 10 to 15% for young men and between 20 to 25% for young women. Body fat percentages greater than 20% for men or 30% for women are considered an indication of obesity.

Thus, overweight and obese should not be used interchangeably. The dissociation between being overweight and obese was demonstrated as far back as the 1940s when researchers studied a group of professional football players. When they compared the players' weights to early actuary weight tables, the majority of the players were considered seriously overweight. But when they tested the players' body compositions, the majority of them had body fat percentages under 20%, meaning that they simply did not fit the "normal" standards for the weight charts.

Health Implications Of Obesity

The evidence is now overwhelming that obesity, defined as excessive storage of energy in the form of fat, has adverse effects on health and longevity. Obesity is clearly associated with hypertension, high cholesterol, diabetes and excess of certain cancers and other medical problems.

Fat Distribution

Obesity is clearly associated with increased medical and health risks. However, exactly where the excess fat is stored is also related to overall mortality and increased risk for cardiovascular disease. In general, women tend to store fat in the lower half of the body around the hip and thigh area (gynoid obesity), whereas men tend to store fat on the upper part of the body around the abdominal area (android obesity). This is the so-called spare tire. Android obesity compared to gynoid obesity is associated with greater risk of developing diabetes, hypertension, heart disease, and death.

Causes of Obesity

The causes of obesity are multifaceted. The diagnosis and treatment of obesity, although a daily occurrence for many physicians, is difficult. The frustrations of obesity are usually evident in both the patient and the physician. A detailed medical and dietary history is important to get before a physician can begin to determine the cause(s) of obesity in patients. Physicians frequently do not spend enough time listening to their patients. In many cases obesity is caused by complex psycho-social issues, which may require a referral to a psychologist or psychiatrist. Many people still feel that obesity is simply caused by eating too much. Although caloric consumption and physical activity habits are directly related to increased prevalence of excess weight, they are not the only causes of obesity.

Metabolic Rate

The thermic effect of food represents approximately 10% of total energy needs. It appears that some individuals may not be as efficient in the way they utilize food when it is digested. One theory that may help explain this imbalance may be found in Brown Fat. Brown fat uses excess food to make heat. Thus, lean individuals may have higher percentages of brown fat compared to obese individuals.

Diet

Most obese individuals tend to not only eat more than lean people, but they also tend to eat foods that are higher in fat and lower in complex carbohydrates. When comparing a group of lean and obese individuals, the lean group derived 29% of their energy from fat and 53% from carbohydrates, versus 35% and 46% respectively for the obese group, even though there was no difference between groups in energy intake. As the percentage of body fat increased, the percentage of energy derived from fat increased, and calories from carbohydrates decreased.

Physical Inactivity

There is substantial evidence that most obesity is caused by physical inactivity versus overeating. A number of scientific studies have demonstrated that sedentary men and women who start a regular exercise program lose body fat, while at the same time increasing their caloric intake. This means that they are now burning energy more efficiently. Individuals who are habitually inactive tend to be at greater risk for obesity. Remember, as we get older our metabolic rate decreases approximately 3 percent per year. If you don't exercise, but continue to consume a normal diet, it is inevitable that you will gain weight. When comparing the habits of lean versus obese individuals, the obese individuals tend to exercise less than the lean group.

Dieting

Caloric restriction, without exercise, has detrimental effects on metabolic rate. When the body senses a reduction in calories being consumed, it automatically slows the metabolic rate down in an effort to conserve energy. So if one is trying to lose weight, dieting alone is one of the worst ways to lose weight. That's why diets don't work. Frequent dieting, also called "yo-yo" dieting, or "weight cycling" has actually been shown to increase the prevalence of obesity. After each diet cycle, the rate of weight loss is slower and weight gain faster.

Weight Loss

Dieting has become a national pasttime for Americans. And even though most people know that dieting alone is ineffective in achieving long-term success, dieting is still the method of choice for most overweight individuals. It has been estimated that at any given time as many as 40% of adult women and 20% of adult men report they are trying to lose weight.

In 1992, the Food and Drug Administration (FDA) and the National Heart, Lung, and Blood Institute (NHLBI) set out to determine the weight loss practices of U.S. adults. The results of this survey found that U.S. adults participate in a wide range of weight loss methods, from diet and exercise, to appetite suppressant pills. Frequently reported weight loss practices included weighing oneself regularly (71% and 70% for women and men, respectively), walking (58% and 44%), using diet soft drinks (52% and 45%), taking vitamins and minerals (33% and 26%), counting calories (25% and 17%), skipping meals (21% and 20%), using commercial meal replacements (15% and 13%), taking diet pills (14% and 7%) and participating in organized weight-loss programs (13% and 5%). Some bright news included the fact that 2/3 of the respondents combined diet and exercise in their plan to lose weight. The unfortunate news was that 20% of the respondents were engaged in such weight loss practices such as weight-loss pills, appetite suppressants, fasting, and vomiting after eating. Thirty percent had been on a diet for more than 1 year.

The Energy Balance Equation

Energy in (food) = energy out (work) + energy out (heat) +/- energy stored (fat)

Weight loss and/or gain can be simply represented by the first law of thermodynamics which states that energy is neither created nor destroyed. Food is consumed and used for energy, heat is released as chemical energy, and some energy may be stored for later energy use. The first law of thermodynamics clearly defines the basic principles and limitations of weight loss. Really, the only way to lose excess body fat is to reduce the left side of the equation (eat less) and increase the right side of the equation (exercise more).

Diets—Past, Present, and Future

Type of Diet	Advantages	Disadvantages	Examples
High-Protein, Low-Carbohydrate Diets			
Usually include all the meat, fish, poultry, and eggs you can eat Occasionally permit milk and cheese in limited amounts Prohibit fruits, vegetables, and any bread or cereal products	Rapid initial weight loss because of diuretic effect Very little hunger	Too low in carbohydrates Deficient in many nutrients—vitamin C, vitamin A (unless eggs are included), calcium, and several trace elements High in saturated fat, cholesterol, and total fat Extreme diets of this type could cause death Impossible to adhere to these diets long enough to lose any appreciable amount of weight Dangerous for people with kidney disease Weight lost, which is largely water, is rapidly regained Expensive Unpalatable after first few days Difficult for dieter to eat out	Dr. Stillman's Quick Weight Loss Diet Calories Don't Count, by Dr. Taller Dr. Atkin's Diet Revolution Scarsdale Diet Air Force Diet
Low-Calorie, High-Protein Supplement Diets			
Usually a premeasured powder to be reconstituted with water or a prepared liquid formula	Rapid initial weight loss Easy to prepare—already measured Palatable for first few days Usually fortified to provide recommended amount of micronutrients Must be labeled if >50% protein	Usually prescribed at dangerously low Calorie intake of 300 to 500 Cal Overpriced Low in fiber and bulk—constipating in short amount of time	Metracal Diet Cambridge Diet Liquid Protein Diets Last Chance Diet Oxford Diet
High-Fiber, Low-Calorie Diets			
	High satiety value Provide bulk	Irritating to the lower colon Decreases absorption of trace elements, especially iron Nutritionally deficient Low in protein	Pritikin Diet F Diet Zen Macrobiotic Diet
Protein-Sparing Modified Fats			
<50% protein: 400 Cal	Safe under supervision High-quality protein Minimize loss of lean body mass	Decreases BMR Monotonous Expensive	Optifast Medifast
Premeasured Food Plans			
	Provide prescribed portion sizes—little chance of too small or too large a portion Total food programs Some provide adequate Calories (1200) Nutritionally balanced or supplemented	Expensive Do not retrain dieters in acceptable eating habits Preclude eating out or social eating Often low in bulk Monotonous Low long-term success rates	Nutri-System Carnation Plan

Source: Hahn/Payne. Focus On Health, 1994 — Mosby-Year Book, Inc.

Diets—Past, Present, and Future—cont'd

Type of Diet	Advantages	Disadvantages	Examples
Limited Food Choice Diets	Reduce the number of food choices made by the users Limited opportunity to make mistakes Almost certainly low in Calories after the first few days	Deficient in many nutrients, depending on the foods allowed Monotonous—difficult to adhere to Eating out and eating socially are difficult Do not retrain dieters in acceptable eating habits Low long-term success rates No scientific basis for these diets	Banana and milk diet Grapefruit and cottage cheese diet Kempner rice diet Lecithin, vinegar, kelp, and vitamin B_6 diet Beverly Hills Diet Fit for Life
Restricted Calorie, Balanced Food Plans	Sufficiently low in Calories to permit steady weight loss Nutritionally balanced Palatable Include readily available foods Reasonable in cost Can be adapted from family meals Permit eating out and social eating Promote a new set of eating habits	Do not appeal to people who want a "unique" diet Do not produce immediate and large weight losses	Weight Watchers Diet Prudent Diet (American Heart Association) The I Love New York Diet UCLA Diet Time-Calorie Displacement (TCD) Fit or Fat Target Diet Take Off Pounds Sensibly (TOPS) Overeaters Anonymous
Fasting Starvation Diet	Rapid initial loss	Nutrient deficient Danger of ketosis >60% loss is muscle <40% loss is fat Low long-term success rates	ZIP Diet
High-Carbohydrate Diet	Emphasizes grains, fruits, and vegetables High in bulk Low in cholesterol	Limits milk, meat Nutritionally very inadequate for calcium, iron, and protein	Beverly Hills Diet Quick Weight Loss Diet Pritikin Diet Carbohydrate Cravers

When a diet plan makes a claim about rapid weight loss without exercise or any special foods, remember .... energy is neither created nor destroyed. You can't wish away excess weight, although everyone has made that wish at least once in their lives.

In order to maintain ideal body weight, energy consumed (food consumed daily) needs to equal energy output (daily physical activity habits). When these are equal, one is said to be in energy balance. In order to gain or lose weight, each side of the equation needs to be adjusted. To lose weight, energy consumed needs to be decreased and energy output needs to be increased. Either a decrease of 1,000 kcal or an increase in energy expenditure of 1,000 kcal (or a combination decrease in energy expenditure of 500 kcal and an increase in energy expenditure of 500 kcal) is needed to lose about 2 pounds per week, which is the maximum recommended weight loss for health.

In a recent study on the effect of weight loss by dieting or exercise on resting metabolic rate in overweight men, researchers found that a one year program of weight loss by energy restriction alone produced a significant decline in the RMR compared to weight loss by exercise which did not change resting metabolic rate. It's been estimated that as much as 25% of the weight lost by dieting alone can be from lean body mass. Since lean body mass is a site of high energy expenditure, any loss in lean body mass will have an effect on RMR and weight loss. Exercise has been shown to decrease energy intake in mildly obese women, compared to a group of sedentary controls.

The Role Of Exercise

Exercise alone, or in combination with a sensible diet produces the best long-term weight loss results. Exercise can contribute up to a 300 to 400 kcal deficit per exercise bout. Keeping food intake constant, an exercise program conducted 3 times per week (at a intensity and duration eliciting 300 to 400 kcal/session) could result in a 16 pound weight loss in one year. The benefits of exercise in weight loss and weight control is really quite minimal, but if exercise training is combined with modest caloric restriction, the negative energy balance is even greater. Exercise is important because it helps maintain resting metabolic rate and fat-free mass. Regular exercise may also help control appetite and improve your psychological outlook when trying to lose weight.

A recent study revealed that after 15 weeks of brisk walking 5 times per week for 45 minutes, overweight women showed a decrease in overall body weight but not body fat, indicating that moderate exercise alone may not be enough to affect body composition. It appears that overweight women may not respond to exercise the same way as men do. In a review of literature it was revealed that exercise alone can stimulate weight loss, but not in women. Women are at a disadvantage compared to men when it comes to elevating and maintaining their resting metabolic rate because of their smaller body size, differences in body fat distribution, and lower aerobic capacity. When obese young women were subjected to a negative energy balance of 3,500 kcal/week either through exercise or dieting over a 12 week period, their weight loss was nearly identical, but the rate of body fat loss in the exercise group was significantly greater. Other studies have shown similar results.

It should be apparent now that you have read this chapter that losing weight is not easy, but it can be done if you decrease your caloric intake and increase your energy expenditure. In other words, the more exercise your do, the greater will be your weight loss.

CHAPTER 9

WALKING FOR BETTER CARDIOVASCULAR HEALTH

Cardiovascular disease continues to be the leading cause of death in the Western world. In 1990, diseases of the heart and blood vessels killed 930,000 Americans. From another perspective, more than two of every five Americans die of cardiovascular disease. The good news is that death rates from cardiovascular disease have been on the decline. From 1980 to 1990, death rates from cardiovascular disease have declined 26.7 percent. The reduction in death rates for cardiovascular diseases can be linked to lifestyle changes among Americans and advances in medical treatments. Cardiovascular disease is still a major killer, but fortunately cardiovascular disease is highly preventable.

Although there are a variety of cardiovascular diseases, including hypertension, stroke, congestive heart failure, etc., the majority of cardiovascular deaths are attributed to coronary artery disease. Coronary artery disease (CAD) results from a process known as atherosclerosis. Atherosclerosis causes a narrowing of the coronary arteries, the arteries that supply the heart muscle with blood and oxygen. The narrowing is thought to be caused first by injury to the inner lining of the arteries (caused by high blood pressures, high levels of LDL cholesterol, or other chemical agents, such as those from cigarettes). Once the inner lining has been damaged, plaques (consisting of calcified cholesterol and fat deposits) begin to reduce the diameter of the coronary artery.

The origin of the study of coronary artery disease in the United States began in a small town in Massachusetts. In the late 1940s, residents of Framingham began to be screened in an effort to determine common patterns or risk factors of cardiovascular disease. Since the start of the Framingham study, hundreds of people have been followed over time. As the result of the Framingham study, as well as hundreds of other studies, the risk factors for coronary heart disease are well defined.

Risk Factors for Coronary Heart Disease

Modifiable

CigaretteSmoking
Hypertension
Diabetes mellitus
High cholesterol
Physical Inactivity
Obesity
Stress

Non-Modifiable

Age
Sex
Family History

When coronary blood flow is unable to meet the heart's demand for oxygen, an individual typically feels chest pressure or chest pain. Chest pain caused by lack of blood flow to the heart is characterized by an intense or dull pain in the chest, sometimes radiating into the neck, jaw, or left shoulder or arm. The transient symptoms of inadequate blood flow to the heart are referred to as angina pectoris. Angina pectoris can be caused by a temporary blockage (spasm) or permanent blockage (plaque). A permanent blockage is dangerous because clots can form at these narrowed sections and result in a myocardial infarction (heart attack).

If a permanent blockage is detected in one or more coronary arteries, the typical treatments include medical management, coronary artery bypass grafting (CABG), percutaneous transluminal coronary angioplasty (PTCA), or other new forms or plaque removal, such as coronary laser (burning the plaque) and high speed rotational atherectomy (cutting and removing the plaque), and to a lesser degree, prescription of lifestyle modifications. Coronary artery bypass grafting (a procedure in which veins are harvested from a patient's leg and sewn from the aorta to the coronary artery past the blockage) does appear to prolong life in patients with severe three vessel disease, but in comparison to medical therapy it does not seem to prolong life in those patients with less severe disease. However, total relief of angina typically occurs in 60 to 75% of patients during the first 5 years following a CABG. The use of percutaneous transluminal coronary angioplasty (a procedure which uses a small balloon at the tip of a heart catheter to push open plaques) are on the rise. Unfortunately, approximately 30% of patients receiving a successful PTCA will have a re-occlusion within the first 3 to 6 months. Less severe cases of coronary artery disease are typically treated with lifestyle modification and medical therapy.

So say you have been diagnosed with coronary heart disease. Perhaps your physician has told you that you have a 70% occlusion

Exercise Guidelines For Low-Risk CAD Individuals

1. Know what your risk factors are for heart disease.

2. If you fall into the medium or high-risk categories, you should consult with your physician before being allowed to exercise.

3. If you recently had a heart attack or heart surgery, get medical clearance and guidelines from a physician.

4. Make sure the guidelines from the physician are carefully followed.

5. Monitor your exercise intensity closely. Make sure you stay within your individual heart rate or RPE range.

6. Inform your physician if you have any abnormal signs or symptoms before, during or after exercise.

7. The exercise intensity level should be kept low to start, and gradually increased over time.

8. Dynamic exercise, such as low impact aerobics, walking, etc. is recommended. Isometric exercises should be avoided. Weight training should be prescribed using low resistance and high repetitions.

9. Low-intensity dynamic exercise versus high-intensity, high impact exercise is recommended. The exercise intensity should be gradually increased to 60 to 85% of the heart rate reserve.

10. Try to exercise at least 3 to 4 times per week. Individuals with low functional capacities may benefit from daily exercise.

11. Perform a longer and more gradual warm-up and cool-down (> 10 minutes). Total exercise duration should be gradually increased to 30 to 60 minutes.

in the circumflex artery, and 80% occlusion in the left anterior descending artery (pretty bad). What treatment would you want, CABG, PTCA, or medication? What if someone told you your coronary artery disease could be reversed through lifestyle modification alone, would you be willing to take a chance on it? Can lifestyle changes reverse coronary heart disease? Many experts now believe so.

Role of Exercise In Preventing Heart Disease

Early researchers linked the amount of physical activity at work to the probability of developing heart disease. The more physically active your job, the less risk you had for developing heart disease. Later it was found that the amount of leisure time physical activity is linked to the probability of developing heart disease as well. Regular aerobic exercise tends to lower blood pressure and total cholesterol, raise the good cholesterol HDL, reduce stress and help regulate blood glucose. Thus exercise alone has a powerful effect on reducing risk factors for heart disease. Exercise in combination with other lifestyle changes (i.e. smoking cessation, stress reduction, changes in diet, etc.) has even more of an effect of lowering coronary heart disease risk factors. Besides helping to prevent heart disease, exercise appears to retard or even reverse coronary atherosclerosis.

Reversing Coronary Heart Disease: a historical perspective

For decades physicians denied that coronary heart disease could be cured, let alone reversed. In fact, as late as 1987, the clinical evidence of regression in humans was quite uncertain. Since the mid-80s, clinical evidence has been accumulating demonstrating that human atherosclerosis is not only preventable, but to some extent reversible, or at least the progression can be delayed. Typically, regression or lack of progression is defined via coronary angiography (a procedure where dye is released from a catheter which is advanced from the femoral artery to the coronary arteries, and x-ray pictures of the coronary anatomy are obtained), before and after some type of intervention. The most common interventions include; surgery, lifestyle modification (diet, exercise, stress reduction), diet alone, and lipid lowering medication.

Probably the first published report of reversal of atherosclerosis came from postmortem examinations of World War I causalities killed in battle, and those who died after spending time in war camps. The soldiers who spent time in war camps had significantly less coronary artery disease, thought to be due to the semi-starvation conditions. Less severe coronary artery disease has been demonstrated in persons who have lost significant weight before they died compared to people who died without the weight loss. Also when animals who were fed a high fat diet, but exercised, were compared to animals that ate a high fat diet with no exercise, the animals that exercised showed less severe coronary artery disease. The results were duplicated with persons who followed a structured lifestyle and/or pharmacological interventions, versus those that didn't.

Numerous studies have demonstrated reversal and/or delayed progression of coronary heart disease in both animals and humans. Today, few medical experts would argue that with the right intervention the progression of coronary artery disease can be reversed and/or at least delayed to some degree. Even in the cases where plaque does not reverse, lifestyle intervention can have a protective effect against heart disease. According to John LaRosa from George Washington University, "Even though the opening may not change much, the plaque is stabilized, which reduces the susceptibility to clotting, and thus future heart attack."

So why isn't lifestyle modification a more commonly prescribed intervention? For whatever reason, aggressive lifestyle intervention for the treatment of coronary artery disease still is not popular among most physicians, probably because of liability and/or financial concerns, as well as the poor probability of patient compliance to such interventions. Most physicians you talk to regarding reversing heart disease through lifestyle modification generally feel that more research is needed. One must ask ... how much research is enough?

Reversing Heart Disease: a current perspective

Perhaps the two most recognized names in the "reversing heart disease game" are Herman Hellerstein, M.D. and Dean Ornish, M.D. In his new book *Healing Your Heart: A Proven Program for Reversing Heart Disease* Dr. Hellerstein shares the findings of his 58 year career. Dr. Hellerstein believes that coronary heart disease can be reversed through lifestyle modification. Dr. Hellerstein recommends a seven step program which relies on sensible lifestyle changes that people can easily make and live with. Dr. Hellerstein's recommendations are based on his own research, as well as other major research projects.

Another name which appears frequently when the subject of reversing heart disease comes up, is Dean Ornish, M.D. In Dr. Ornish's new book, *Dr. Dean Ornish's Program for Reversing Heart Disease*, Dr. Ornish claims that he is "the first to scientifically prove heart disease is reversible." In his Lifestyle Heart trial, Dr. Ornish set out to determine the effects of lifestyle modification on coronary heart disease. Dr. Ornish placed 28 patients on a comprehensive lifestyle modification program, while another group of 20 received usual medical care. Both groups had an initial coronary angiogram to assess the amount of blockage, and another one 1 year later. After one year, the group that followed the lifestyle modification program showed a significant overall regression of coronary atherosclerosis as measured by coronary angiography. The other group that was following a less stringent lifestyle modification program showed significant overall "progression" of coronary artery blockage.

Dr. Ornish states that, "A comprehensive lifestyle change may be able to bring about regression of even severe coronary atherosclerosis after only one year, without the use of lipid-lowering drugs." Unlike Dr. Hellerstein, Dr. Ornish believes that, "if you have coronary heart disease, then your intake of fat and cholesterol needs to be very low." The findings of Dr. Ornish's program leads one to believe that conventional dietary recommendations for heart patients (no more than 30% of daily calories from fat) are not sufficient enough to cause regression of coronary heart disease in many patients. Even with such impressive results, most Americans are not willing to follow the strict guidelines of Dr. Ornish. Many researchers and medical experts believe that it doesn't take such a radical diet to start to unclog your arteries.

Dr. Hellerstein's Seven Goals for Reversing Coronary Heart Disease

1. Reduce total cholesterol to below 200 mg/dl and LDL below 130 mg/dl, with a total cholesterol/HDL ratio of 3.5. Diet recommendations — 1,500 to 2,500 calories per day, with saturated fat content under 10% and total fat less than 30% of total calories, 50 to 100 mg cholesterol per day.

2. Achieve a normal blood pressure of 140/90 or better.

3. Burn at least 150 to 300 calories per day through aerobic exercise.

4. Maintain a normal body weight.

5. Reduce the amount of stress in your life.

6. Do not use any tobacco.

7. Maintain normal blood-sugar levels.

It is now quite clear that regular physical activity, including walking, can help reduce your risk for developing coronary artery disease, and if you have disease, possibly reduce the progression of it. Walking is now routinely recommended by physicians to their patients as a way to prevent heart disease and rehabilitate from it, especially after having a heart attack or open heart surgery. But exercise cannot reduce all of your risk. You still need to look at your diet, smoking and stress habits and blood pressure. Without a doubt, regular walking will help you reduce your risk for developing one of the most common medical problems in this country.

Dr. Ornish's Program for Reversing Coronary Heart Disease

1. The Ornish Diet recommendations include:
   - a. low-fat (10% of daily calories)
   - b. low cholesterol (5 mg/day)
   - c. no animal products, except egg whites and one cup of nonfat milk or yogurt.
   - d. high in complex carbohydrates (70-75% of daily calories).
   - e. no caffeine, and no more than 2 units of alcohol per day.

2. No smoking

3. Moderate exercise (3 hours/week for a minimum of 30 minutes per session at an intensity of 50-80% of your training heart rate.

4. One hour per day of stress management techniques, including:
   - a. stretching
   - b. meditation
   - c. progressive relaxation exercises
   - d. deep breathing exercises

CHAPTER 10

SPECIAL CONSIDERATIONS

The benefits of regular physical activity and exercise are becoming increasingly more clear. Individuals who choose to be more physically active in both their leisure and work activities statistically lower their risk for developing degenerative diseases such as osteoporosis, diabetes, obesity and cardiovascular disease, to name a few. The term "health-related fitness" now appears frequently in exercise literature to describe the health benefits of exercise. Instead of defining physical fitness in terms of one's athletic abilities (speed, power, balance, etc.), health-related physical fitness defines an individual's fitness status based on his/her cardiorespiratory fitness, muscular strength, blood pressure, body composition, etc. The shift in emphasis from performance-related fitness to health-related physical fitness has far reaching implications for health and fitness professionals.

Exercise is also becoming increasingly recognized as an important part of therapy in the rehabilitation of certain acute and chronic health conditions. For example, aerobic exercise is widely recommended and supported as an adjunct treatment for individuals recovering from coronary heart disease. Several recent studies have shown that exercise combined with risk factor modification can significantly decrease morbidity and mortality in individuals with known coronary heart disease. Even a modest amount of physical activity, such as daily brisk walking, can reduce the risk of developing heart disease.

Exercise and the Elderly

If you haven't noticed, our population is getting older. By the year 2030 over 20% of our population will be over the age of 65. This age group represents the fastest growing segment of our population. Aging is a normal biological process. Even though certain physiological changes are inevitable with aging, it appears that the effects of aging can be reduced or even postponed through exercise. No one can promise that exercise will prolong life, but research is certainly suggesting that one's quality of life can be improved through regular exercise.

Normal Physiological Changes With Aging and The Response To Exercise

Heart Rate — Maximal heart rate is age related. With age, maximal heart rate declines. The accuracy of estimating training intensity based on heart rate diminishes with age. Other methods of monitoring exercise intensity, such as the rate of perceived exertion scale, should be considered when working with the elderly. Even though exercise heart rate declines with age, in healthy older subjects who exercise, stroke volume (or the amount of blood pumped out of the heart per beat) has been shown to increase, and thus overcome the effect of a lowered heart rate.

Maximal Oxygen Uptake — With normal aging, maximal oxygen uptake declines approximately eight to ten percent per decade after age thirty. This decline is primarily due to the decrease in maximal heart rate. It is clear however, that aerobic capacity can be improved at any age. In one study, a group of 49 to 65 year old sedentary men walked and jogged three times a week for 20 weeks. Following the training, the men had improved their aerobic capacity by an average of 18 percent. In another study, a 22 percent increase in aerobic capacity was found in a group of 70 to 79 year old participants. Reduction in aerobic capacity can be altered by exercise training.

Bones — Our bones become more fragile with age. Serious and often debilitating fractures are common in the elderly. By the age of 90, as many as 32 percent of women and 17 percent of men will have sustained a hip fracture, and between 12 and 20 percent of this group will die of related complications. Osteoporosis, or a gradual loss or thinning of bone with aging, is a major concern to the elderly. Weight bearing and resistance training exercises are known to help maintain bone mass. The positive effect of exercise in preventing osteoporosis is based on extensive literature documenting the rapid onset and severe bone loss in immobilized individuals and the significant difference in bone density (bone strength) of physically active versus sedentary individuals. Regular physical activity appears to have beneficial effects on the rate of age-related bone loss.

Skeletal Muscle — Muscle mass declines with age, resulting in decreased muscular strength and endurance. For each decade after the age of 25, three to five percent of muscle mass is lost. Significant strength gains are possible in the elderly. The result from a 1988 Tufts University study found that in a group of 60 to 72 year-old untrained men, participating in 12 weeks of strength training (8 repetitions/set, 3 sets/day, 3 days/week), showed a 107% increase in knee extensor strength and a 227% increase in knee flexor strength following 12 weeks of training. This study demonstrated that strength gains do occur in older men, and these gains are associated with significant muscle hypertrophy and muscle protein turnover.

Flexibility — With normal aging, connective tissue becomes stiffer, and joints become less mobile. Loss of flexibility with age may also be the result of underlining degenerative disease processes such as arthritis. Flexibility does decrease with age; however, there is no evidence that the biological processes associated with aging are responsible for this loss. Loss of flexibility is more likely the result of diminishing physical activity. Flexibility can be improved at any age through exercises that promote the elasticity of the soft tissues.

Body Composition — Lean body weight declines and body fat increases with normal aging. The changes in body composition resulting from age are primarily due to a decrease in the basal metabolic rate and physical activity habits of elderly. Basal metabolic rate declines at a rate of 3 percent per decade. Numerous studies have demonstrated the beneficial effects of exercise on body composition in the elderly.

Exercice Guidelines For Seniors

1. Particular care should be taken when lifting weights.
2. An extended cool-down period, approximately 10 to 15 minutes, is recommended.
3. The elderly often have a more difficult time when exercising in extreme environmental conditions. Avoid exercising in these conditions if possible.
4. Some elderly individuals with arthritis or poor joint mobility may have to participate in non-weight bearing activities, such as cycling, swimming and chair and floor exercises.
5. The exercise intensity level should be kept low to start, and gradually increased over time.
6. Dynamic exercise, such as low impact aerobics, walking, etc., is recommended. Isometric exercises should be avoided. Weight training should be prescribed using low resistance and high repetitions.
7. Low-intensity dynamic exercise versus high-intensity, high impact exercise is recommended. The exercise intensity should be gradually increased to 60% to 85% of the heart rate reserve.
8. Try to exercise at least 3 to 4 times per week. Individuals with low functional capacities may benefit from daily exercise.

Children

There is an abundance of literature citing the poor physical fitness and health status of American children. One of the most alarming statistics comes from the National Children and Youth Fitness Study, which reported that approximately 20% of this nation's children and adolescents between the ages of 5 and 17 are considered obese. This figure is 50% higher than 20 years ago. And unfortunately, obese children have a much higher probability of becoming obese adults. Another alarming health statistic reports that as many as 40% of children between the ages of 5 and 8 already exhibit at least one of the following heart disease risk factors; obesity, hypertension, and high cholesterol levels.

It is important to get children interested and involved in exercise sport activities at an early age. Exercise and fitness activities should be enjoyable, and appropriate for the age of the child. The more parents get involved, the more likely children are to be physically active. The National Youth Fitness Study found that while schools are important to a child's exercise and health habits, home and community environments contribute in a significant way. Children who watch more television, have less active parents, and participate less in community activities tend to score lower on health-related fitness measures.

Exercise training should be considered an important part of health promotion efforts for children. Physical activity needs to become a lifetime pursuit. Educators, parents and fitness professionals can help achieve this goal by teaching children positive attitudes, that fitness is fun, and by making children aware of the benefits of exercise at a young age. Within the last decade, a great deal of research has focused on the effects of exercise training in children. From these studies, it appears that children respond to training much the same way as adults do. Studies have demonstrated that important health and performance characteristics can be improved through exercise.

Endurance Training Guidelines

Sufficient evidence exists that children physiologically adapt to endurance training. Lacking, however, is a general consensus on the quality and quantity of exercise required to improve and maintain a minimum level of fitness in children. Recommendations for adults have been published by the American College of Sports Medicine in their position stand. In 1988, the American College of Sports Medicine published an opinion statement on physical fitness in children and youth. They state that, "until more definitive evidence is available, current recommendations are that children and youth obtain 20-30 minutes of vigorous exercise each day."

General Exercise Training Guidelines for Children

1. Although children are generally quite active, they generally choose to participate in activities that consist of short-burst, high-energy exercise. Children should be encouraged to participate in sustained activities that use large muscle groups.

2. The type, intensity and duration of exercise activities need to be based on the maturity of the child, medical status, and previous experiences with exercise.

3. Regardless of age, the exercise intensity should start out low and progress gradually.

4. Children are involved in a variety of activities throughout the day. Because of this, a specific time should be dedicated to sustained aerobic activities.

5. The duration of the exercise session will vary depending on the age of the children, their previous exercise experience, and the intensity of the exercise session.

6. Because it is often quite difficult to get children to respond to sustained periods of exercise, the session periods need to be creatively designed.

7. Children should be encouraged to participate in sustained activities that use large muscle groups (i.e. swimming, jogging, aerobic dance, etc.). Other activities, such as recreational, sport and fun activities that develop other components of fitness (speed, power, flexibility, muscular endurance, agility and coordination) should be incorporated into a fitness program.

8. The exercise intensity should start out low, and progress gradually. There are currently no universal recommendations available for the use of training heart rate during exercise for children.

9. Two to three days of endurance training will allow adequate time to participate in other activities, and yet be sufficient enough to cause a training effect.

10. Since children will be involved in a variety of activities during and after school, a specific amount of time should be dedicated to endurance training. Endurance exercise activities should be gradually increased to 30 to 40 minutes per session. With younger children, it will be necessary to start out with less time initially.

Exercise During Pregnancy

Exercise has become a way of life for millions of women. In the United States alone, there are over 2 million women that run or walk an average of 3 to 4 days per week. A large percentage of these women are exercising during their reproductive years. Many of them will someday decide to get pregnant. At some point during the initial stages of their pregnancy, they must make a decision whether or not they will continue to exercise during their pregnancy. For those dedicated exercisers contemplating having to give up exercise during pregnancy — wait, you may not have to. Running and walking are becoming increasingly more accepted as a safe form of exercise during pregnancy.

Women in good physical condition prior to becoming pregnant should be able to continue to exercise during pregnancy with little difficulty. However, starting a vigorous exercise program during pregnancy is not safe. Pregnancy is not a time to get serious about fitness. Many women try to get in shape during their pregnancies in an effort to prepare for the birth and to recover faster. Such activities are not safe, and predispose the mother and infant to potential injury. The most important goal of exercising during pregnancy and the postpartum period should be to maintain the highest level of fitness consistent with maximum safety. Women who exercise regularly should feel more confident before and during labor, for their high endurance level will help them cope with the physical demands of labor and delivery.

The scientific study of exercise and pregnancy is in its infancy, and thus, there is still a great deal we don't know. Most of the research dealing with exercise and pregnancy has focused on the mother, since it is much easier and safer. Research focusing on the effects of the fetus have primarily come from studies done on pregnant sheep, goats and rats, and thus it is difficult to make accurate estimates of the effects on humans.

The cardiovascular responses of pregnant women have been studied extensively. Numerous studies have demonstrated that women can improve and maintain their cardiovascular, respiratory and aerobic capacities during pregnancy. Other research has looked at the effect exercise has on the fetus. Since exercise causes redistribution of blood flow to the working muscles, exercising during pregnancy may cause a reduction of blood flow to the uterus, and possibly harm the developing fetus. However, several recent studies have shown that, while there is a slight decrease in overall uterine blood flow during moderate exercise, blood flow to the placenta appears to be adequate.

Cardiac reserve, or the difference between resting and maximum cardiac function, is reduced in pregnant women. There is evidence that as pregnancy progresses, the heart is less able to adapt to the increased demand. The cardiovascular systems of pregnant women may be already working a very high level, due to the increased demands of the pregnancy. This is the best evidence to discourage pregnant women from exercising at high levels or participating in activities that require sudden bursts of movement.

Many women feel they are more flexible during pregnancy. This increased flexibility is due to joint laxity. With the release of the hormone relaxin, joints become looser, and there is increased risk for potential injury during running. Pregnant women that run during pregnancy are at greater risk for sprains and strains due to joint laxity, postural changes associated with pregnancy, and the increased tendency to have minor accidents during pregnancy.

Recent studies have reported runners who continue to run during pregnancy have quite normal births. One study found that running during pregnancy caused earlier deliveries (by 8 days) and lighter-weight babies (1.3 to 1.5 pounds lighter) than sedentary women or women who stopped exercising altogether. (It should be noted that a smaller baby does not mean an unhealthy baby) However, in a similar study based on responses of 195 female runners, birth weights and deliveries were not significantly different from non-exercising women. In one study where pregnant women averaged

1.5 to 2.5 miles per day reported that the number of problem pregnancies was no higher in the running population than in the general population.

Women that choose to exercise during pregnancy need to be especially aware of the ambient temperature prior to beginning their run. Exercise causes an increase in body temperature, which can be harmful to the fetus if the core body temperature exceeds 100° F. Pregnant women should be conservative when running in hot, humid environments, since body temperature regulation becomes more difficult. If the mother becomes overheated due to higher temperature or humidity during running, she may not be able to dissipate fetal heat, which could be detrimental to the fetus.

Most women should be able to continue to walk or run during their first trimester without much difficulty. Other than morning sickness, mild weight gain, and an increased feeling of fatigue, most women should be able to continue their normal exercise program. During the second and third trimesters of pregnancy, running may become more difficult due to increased body weight, lower limb swelling, varicose veins and increased joint mobility due to hormonal changes and connective tissue changes. Thus walking is recommended.

The decision to walk vigorously during pregnancy should be a joint decision that is made between the mother and the primary care physician. Women should clearly understand the risks and potential benefits associated with exercising during pregnancy.

Although there are no official standards for exercise during pregnancy, the American College of Obstetricians and Gynecologists' position statement maintains that current research indicates that exercise during pregnancy is safe, assuming that the participants are carefully monitored by their physician and they understand the special precautions that need to be followed while exercising during pregnancy.

Running and walking during pregnancy appear to be safe for the mother and the fetus. As long as women are generally healthy prior to conception, adhere to the guidelines and recommendations mentioned above, and keep their physician informed as to their mileage or exercise time, exercise should be an enjoyable experience during pregnancy. Walking during pregnancy will allow the mother to maintain her fitness level through the birth, and allow her to recover faster as well.

General Guidelines For Exercising During Pregnancy

1. Discuss your exercise goals during pregnancy with your physician.
2. Do not begin a vigorous exercise program before becoming pregnant, or while pregnant.
3. Gradually reduce your mileage or exercise time during the second and third trimesters. (Example — a woman averaging 4 miles of walking a day might reduce her mileage down to 3 miles per day on average during the first trimester, down to 2 miles in the second and finally to 1 to 1.5 during the third.
4. Avoid walking when the temperature and/or humidity is high.
5. Try to walk on flat, even surfaces.
6. Gradually reduce the intensity of exercise sessions as well. Walking during pregnancy is not a time to engage in competitive activities; rather, it is a time to maintain fitness.
7. If running becomes uncomfortable during the second and third trimesters, try other forms of aerobic exercise, including; swimming, running in water, bicycling, aerobic dance classes, etc..
8. Extend warm-up and cool-down periods.
9. Initially, body temperature should be taken immediately after exercise, and should not exceed 101 degrees. If body temperature exceeds 101 degrees, modifications in exercise intensity and duration, as well as timing exercise sessions for the cooler part of the day, should help.

10. Women are encouraged to use perceived exertion ratings, versus fixed heart rates to monitor exercise intensity. Women should run at a pace that is comfortable. A pounding heart rate, breathlessness or dizziness are signs to reduce walking pace.
11. Eat a small snack before running to help avoid hypoglycemia.
12. Drink plenty of water before, during and after walking.
13. Do not overstretch, or move in a range of motion that is different from what is normally performed.
14. Report to your doctor immediately, any unusual changes (vaginal bleeding, severe fatigue, joint pain, irregular heart beats, etc..).
15. Wear more supportive/protective shoes while walking or running during pregnancy.

Exercise and Hypertension

Hypertension is one of the most prevalent chronic diseases in the United States, affecting more than 30% of all Americans. Hypertension is a condition in which the blood pressure is chronically elevated above levels desirable for an individual's age and health. Hypertension is defined as 140/90 mm Hg for individuals younger than 60 or greater than 160/95 mm Hg for those older than 60. Half of all individuals with high blood pressure don't even know they have it, that is why hypertension is commonly referred to as the "silent killer." It is a serious health problem because people affected by high blood pressure have three to four times the risk of developing coronary heart disease and up to seven times the risk of having a stroke.

The Role Of Exercise In Hypertension Control

Exercise training is now recognized as an important part of therapy for controlling hypertension. Several exercise training studies have confirmed that regular physical activity results in lower blood pressure readings compared to sedentary individuals. The reduction in blood pressure following endurance exercise appears to be related to the widening of the blood vessels that exercise causes, which results in a reduction in vascular resistance, as well as the reduction of heart rate at rest. Since most hypertensive clients are obese, non-drug therapy is usually the first line of treatment. A combination of weight reduction, salt restriction and increased physical activity have all been recommended as treatments for reducing and controlling high blood pressure.

Exercise Guidelines for Hypertensive Individuals

1. Avoid holding your breath and straining during exercise (Valsalva maneuver).
2. If you exercise with weights, the resistance should be kept low and the repetitions high.
3. Exercise intensity may need to be monitored by the RPE scale, since medications can affect the heart rate during exercise.
4. Inform your physician if you experience any abnormal signs or symptoms before, during, or immediately following exercise.
5. You should monitor and track your blood pressure before and after exercise.
6. Move slowly when transitioning from the floor to standing, since hypertensive individuals are more susceptible to dizziness if on antihypertensive medication.
7. The exercise intensity level should be kept low to start, and gradually increased over time.
8. Dynamic exercise, such as low impact aerobics, walking, etc., is recommended. Isometric exercises should be avoided. Weight training should be prescribed using low resistance and high repetitions.
9. The intensity should be gradually increased to 60 to 85% of the heart rate reserve.
10. Try to to exercise at least 3 to 4 times per week. Individuals with low functional capacities may benefit from daily exercise.
11. Perform a longer and more gradual warm-up and cool-down (> 10 minutes). Total exercise duration should be gradually increased to 30 to 60 minutes.

Coronary Artery Disease

Coronary artery disease continues to be the leading cause of death in the United States. The majority of heart attacks are caused by the build-up of plaque in the arteries supplying blood to the heart muscle (coronary arteries). This process is referred to as atherosclerosis. The plaque consists of fatty substances, cholesterol and other blood and chemical substances. The plaque enlarges over time, progressively narrowing the arterial channel through which blood travels. Eventually a clot forms and completely closes the vessel, resulting in a heart attack.

Exercise plays an important role in preventing heart disease, as well as in the rehabilitation of individuals with heart disease. The major risk factors for coronary heart disease — hypertension, smoking, high cholesterol — are all positively affected by exercise. Furthermore, physical inactivity is now recognized as a major contributor to the atherosclerotic process. Coronary heart disease can be delayed or prevented by keeping risk factors controlled.

The Role of Exercise In Preventing and Treating CAD

The benefits of habitual physical activity on preventing and treating coronary heart disease are becoming increasingly more clear. In fact, physical inactivity is now recognized as a major contributor to the heart disease process. Numerous studies have confirmed that even moderate exercise can produce favorable improvements in cardiorespiratory endurance and reduced CAD risk factors.

Exercise Guidelines For Low-Risk CAD Individuals

1. Know what your risk factors are for heart disease.
2. If you fall into the medium or high-risk categories, you should consult with your physician before being allowed to exercise.
3. If you recently had a heart attack or heart surgery, get medical clearance and guidelines from a physician.
4. Make sure the guidelines from the physician are carefully followed.
5. Monitor your exercise intensity closely. Make sure you stay within your individual heart rate or RPE range.
6. Inform your physician if you have any abnormal signs or symptoms before, during or after exercise.
7. The exercise intensity level should be kept low to start, and gradually increased over time.
8. Dynamic exercise, such as low impact aerobics, walking, etc., are recommended. Isometric exercises should be avoided. Weight training should be prescribed using low resistance and high repetitions.
9. Low-intensity dynamic exercise versus high-intensity, high impact exercise is recommended. The exercise intensity should be gradually increased to 60% to 85% of the heart rate reserve.
10. Try to exercise at least 3 to 4 times per week. Individuals with low functional capacities may benefit from daily exercise.
11. Perform a longer and more gradual warm-up and cool-down (> 10 minutes). Total exercise duration should be gradually increased to 30 to 60 minutes.

Diabetes

Diminished secretion of insulin by the pancreas or an inability to utilize insulin results in a disease known as diabetes mellitus. Diabetes is a serious disease if left untreated. Diabetics are at greater risk for numerous health problems including kidney failure, nerve disorders, eye problems and heart disease. Prolonged and frequent elevation of blood sugar can lead to microangiopathy, a term that refers to damaged capillaries, which in-turn leads to poor circulation. In addition, diabetics are at greater risk for developing neuropathy, a term referring to damaged nerves, which can lead to permanent nerve damage.

There are two forms of diabetes, insulin dependent (Type I) and non-insulin dependent (Type II). Type I diabetes is caused by destruction of the insulin producing beta cells in the pancreas. Type I diabetics produce little or no insulin. Type I diabetes generally occurs in childhood, and regular insulin injections are required to regulate blood glucose levels. Type II diabetes is the most common form of diabetes, affecting 90% of all diabetic patients. Type II diabetes typically occurs in adults that are overweight. Type II diabetics are not able to use the insulin they produce because of reduced sensitivity of their insulin target cells. Treatment of Type II diabetes varies and may include a change in diet, medication and exercise therapy.

Effective Diabetic Control

Effective diabetic control is based on long-term regulation of blood glucose levels. Glucose regulation in Type I diabetics is achieved through regular glucose assessment, proper diet, exercise and appropriate insulin medication. For the Type II diabetic, glucose regulation is achieved through a change in lifestyle centered around proper diet, weight loss/control, exercise, and insulin or oral agents if needed. A combined diet and exercise regime results in weight loss and weight control, improvement in cardiorespiratory fitness, reduced need for insulin, improved self-image and better ability to deal with stress.

The Role Of Exercise In Diabetic Control

Exercise plays an important role in diabetic control. One of the major benefits of exercise for diabetics is that it makes the muscle cells more permeable to glucose. Aerobic exercise seems to have an insulin-like effect, allowing the body to make better use of available insulin. Another important benefit of aerobic exercise is the effect it has on reducing cholesterol levels and weight. With excessive blood glucose elevation, blood fats rise to become the primary energy source for the body. Since diabetics are prone to having higher than normal blood fat levels, they are also at higher risk for heart disease.

Exercise Program Design Considerations

Before beginning an exercise program, diabetics need to speak with their physician or diabetes educator so that a program of diet, exercise and medication can be developed. The primary goal of exercise for the Type I diabetic should be better glucose regulation and reduced heart disease risk. For the insulin dependent diabetic the timing of exercise, the amount of insulin injected, and the injection site are important considerations before exercising. Exercise should be performed daily so that a regular pattern of diet and insulin dosage can be maintained. Since the frequency and duration of exercise are lower for the Type I diabetic, the intensity can be slightly higher than the Type II diabetic.

The primary goal of exercise for the Type II diabetic is weight loss and control. Eighty percent of Type II diabetics are overweight. By losing weight through the combined effect of diet and exercise, Type II diabetics will reduce the amount of oral insulin medication needed. The primary objective during exercise for the Type II diabetic is caloric expenditure. Maximizing caloric expenditure is best achieved by low intensity, long duration exercise. Since the frequency and duration of exercise are high for Type II diabetics, the intensity of exercise should be kept low.

Exercise Guidelines for Type I and Type II Diabetics

1. Diabetics requiring insulin injections should not inject in primary muscle groups that will be used during exercise. This regime can cause the insulin to be absorbed too quickly, resulting in hypoglycemia.

2. Diabetics need to check their blood glucose levels frequently. Patients should work with their physician to determine the right insulin dosage, based in part on the blood glucose levels before and after exercise.

3. Diabetics should be encouraged to always carry a rapid-acting carbohydrate (such as juice or candy) to correct for hypoglycemia.

4. Diabetics should be encouraged to exercise at the same time every day for better control.

5. Exercise should be avoided during peak insulin activity.

6. Carbohydrate snacks should be consumed before and during prolonged exercise.

7. Diabetics need to take very good care of their feet. Diabetics need to regularly check for any cuts, blisters or signs of infection. Good quality exercise shoes are also very important.

Sample Exercise Prescription

	Type I	Type II
Mode:	Aerobic	Aerobic
Intensity:	Low to High	Low
Frequency:	5-7 days/week	4-5 days/week
Duration:	20-40 minutes	40-60 minutes

Special Precautions

For the Type I diabetic, two potential problems can occur during or following exercise. First, lack of insulin may cause a hyperglycemic effect. Hyperglycemia occurs when there is insufficient insulin to mobilize glucose and glucose levels become elevated to dangerous levels. A second potential problem that can occur is when insulin is mobilized too quickly, thus lowering the blood glucose to a dangerous level. A low blood glucose level is referred to as hypoglycemia.

One of the first rules for the insulin dependent diabetic is to either reduce insulin intake or increase carbohydrate intake before exercise.

For both types of diabetics, exercise should begin 1 to 2 hours after a meal, and before peak insulin activity. Usually insulin dosages must be decreased prior to exercise, since exercise has an insulin-like effect.

The golden rules of glucose regulation during exercise are to check blood glucose levels frequently when starting an exercise program, and be aware of any unusual symptoms prior to, during or after exercise.

Asthma

Asthma is a reactive airway disease characterized by shortness of breath, coughing and wheezing. It is due to constriction of the smooth muscle around the airways, a swelling of the mucosal cells and increased secretion of mucus. Asthma can be caused by an allergic reaction, exercise, infections, emotion or other environmental irritants. Approximately 80% of asthmatics experience asthma attacks during exercise, a term referred to as exercise induced asthma (EIA). Asthma is not inhibitive to exercise, however. Before starting an exercise program, asthmatics should develop a plan for exercise with their physician.

The Role of Exercise and Asthma

Individuals with controlled asthma should benefit from regular exercise. Although asthmatics are more likely to experience breathlessness during exercise, this should not stop them from exercising. During exercise, some asthmatics will get short of breath due to the cooling effect in the airways caused by the large volumes of inspired air and also because of the evaporation of water in the respiratory tract.

Special Precautions

- Patients with respiratory disorders need to be carefully followed by a physician.

- Only patients with stable asthma should exercise.

- If an asthma attack is not relieved by medication, get to a medical facility immediately or call an ambulance.

Exercise Guidelines For Asthmatics

1. Before starting an exercise program, asthmatics must have a medication plan to prevent EIA attacks.
2. Asmatics should have a bronchodilating inhaler with them at all times, and be instructed to use it at the first sign of wheezing.
3. The exercise intensity should be kept low to begin with, and gradually increased over time.
4. The exercise intensity should be reduced if asthma symptoms occur.
5. Using an inhaler several minutes before exercise may reduce the possibility of an EIA attack.
6. Drink plenty of fluids before and during exercise.
7. An extended warm-up and cool-down period should be encouraged with asthmatics.
8. Individuals with respiratory disorders will often experience more symptoms of respiratory distress when exercising in extreme environmental conditions (high or low temperature, high pollen count and heavy air pollution).
9. Dynamic exercise, walking, cycling and swimming is recommended. Upper body exercises such as arm cranking, rowing and cross-country skiing may not be appropriate because of the higher ventilation demands.
10. Low-intensity dynamic exercise versus high-intensity, high impact exercise is recommended.
11. Asthmatics should be encouraged to exercise at least 3 to 4 times per week. Asthmatics with low functional capacities or who experience shortness of breath during prolonged exercise, may benefit from intermittent exercise (two 10 minute sessions).

Low Back Pain

Back injuries, including sprains and strains, are the number one disability for people under age 45. It has been estimated that 80% of the population will experience an episode of low back pain some time in their lives. Of the 80%, 5% will go on to develop chronic low back pain. Low back pain (LBP) accounts for 10% of all chronic health conditions in the U.S. and 25% of days lost from work. LBP has been referred to by medical experts as the most expensive benign health condition in America.

Back injuries translate into millions of lost work days every year and cost billions for medical care, disability payments and legal payments. Reducing back injury rates is a top priority for all employers. In fact, the most common type of workers' compensation claim is a back strain/sprain, which accounts for up to 25% of all claims, representing annual payments of $2.5 to 7 billion, including one-half of all disability compensation payments annually! In addition, nearly 2% of the U.S. workforce file back compensation claims.

The Role of Exercise In Preventing and Treating LBP

It appears that physical fitness combined with a healthy lifestyle may help prevent low back pain. In fact many physicians feel that the major cause of chronic low back pain is simply physical deconditioning. More specifically, low endurance of large muscle groups, particularly the back extensors, seems to put one at a greater risk of developing low back pain. Exercises for the lower back should be performed on a regular basis to gain maximal benefits.

Special Precautions

- Begin and stay with an organized program of physical exercise emphasizing general fitness, aerobic capacity and specific reconditioning of the muscles that support the spine. Before and after participating in any sport, remember to do warm-up and cool-down exercises.
- Learn to match your lifting capacity to the requirements of your job. Remember that moving large bulky objects is as stressful as moving small heavy objects. Keep the load close to the body, and always face the work.
- Avoid activities that are clearly associated with previous episodes of low back pain.
- Whenever possible, use lifting tables and other lifting devices.
- Adjust table heights to a comfortable level.
- Use back rests and lumbar supports when sitting.
- Change your position (for example, from sitting to standing) regularly.
- Make sure your car or truck seats offer optimal seating comfort.
- Quit smoking.
- Reduce stress and anxiety.
- Enroll in a class to learn more about preventing LBP.

Exercise Guidelines for Low Back Pain Sufferers

1. Always be aware of proper form and alignment when exercising.
2. Always maintain pelvic neutral alignment and an erect torso during any exercise movements.
4. When leaning forward, lifting or lowering an object, always bend at the knees.
5. Avoid hyperextending the spine in an unsupported position.
6. Allow for an adequate warm-up and cool-down period during all exercise sessions.
7. Most low back pain is caused by muscle weaknesses and imbalances including tight hamstring and lower back muscle groups, tight hip flexor muscles, and weak abdominal and lower back muscles. Exercises should be routinely performed to improve muscle strength and flexibility.
8. Individuals who experience low back pain or have a history of chronic low back pain should consult with a physician and get specific recommendations for exercises.

Arthritis

Although there are different forms of arthritis, the most common forms are rheumatoid and osteoarthritis. Osteoarthritis is a degenerative process caused by the wearing away of cartilage, leaving two surfaces of bone in contact with each other. Rheumatoid arthritis is caused by an inflammation of the membrane surrounding joints. It is often associated with pain and swelling in one or more joints. The benefits of exercise include stronger muscles and bones, improved cardiorespiratory fitness, and improved psychosocial well-being. Exercise is not advisable during inflammatory periods because exercise can worsen the process.

The Role of Exercise for Arthritic Patients

Exercise is recommended for patients with arthritis to help preserve muscle strength and joint mobility, to improve functional capabilities, to relieve pain and stiffness, to prevent further deformities, to improve overall physical conditioning, to re-establish neuromuscular coordination and to mobilize stiff or contracted joints. Improvement of function and pain relief are the ultimate goals.

Exercise Guidelines For Arthritis Sufferers

1. Individuals with arthritis should be encouraged to participate in exercise where quick or excessive movement can be avoided, such as walking or water exercise classes.
2. Exercise sessions should begin at a low-intensity with frequent sessions.
3. The exercise intensity and duration should be reduced during periods of inflammation or pain.
4. Arthritic individuals may need an extended warm-up and cool-down period.
5. The exercise session should be modified in terms of intensity and duration according to how well an arthritic individual responds, changes in medication and the disease and pain levels.
6. Try to tailor your stretching to focus on the arthritic joints.
7. Take a day or two of rest if you continue to experience pain during or following an exercise session.
8. Always concentrate on proper body alignment during exercise.
9. Poor posture can predispose you to muscle aches and pains that will limit the amount of exercise you can perform.
10. Pain is quite normal in people with arthritis. Try to work just up to the point of pain, but not past it. Simple movements for healthy people can be quite painful for individuals with arthritis.
11. It is essential to put all joints through a range of motion at least once a day to maintain mobility.
12. Non-weight bearing activities such as cycling and swimming are preferred because they reduce joint stress.
13. Low-intensity dynamic exercise versus high-intensity, high impact exercise is recommended. The exercise intensity should be carefully prescribed based on pain tolerance before, during and after exercise.
14. Try to exercise at least 4 to 5 times per week. Arthritic individuals usually benefit from frequent exercise sessions (daily).

CHAPTER 11

NUTRITION TIPS

Proper nutrition is essential to good health. Good nutrition promotes normal growth and development and can help prevent disease. Today in most developed countries, good nutritional habits have helped prevent a variety of diseases and health-related problems. Diseases such as rickets, scurvy and goiters (which are caused by a lack of certain vitamins) were once common, but are now quite rare. Living in a developed country like the United States does not guarantee that a health supporting diet will always be achieved. There are many Americans that are undernourished due to social status, medical/health problems, or for self-imposed reasons. This can result in retardation of growth, anemia and other serious health problems. However, there are far more people that are overnourished than are undernourished. Even with increased awareness and education on nutrition and exercise, most people find it hard to eat balanced, nutritious meals and exercise on a regular basis.

The three basic foods, carbohydrates, fats, and proteins, provide the energy for every function of the human body. A health supporting diet is composed of 55% to 60% carbohydrates, 25% to 30% fat, and 10% to 15% protein. The best way to eat a balanced diet is to eat a variety of foods. A balanced meal offers protein, fat and carbohydrates all together. The Food Guide Pyramid has been developed to help you make the right nutritional choices.

Carbohydrates

Carbohydrates are often referred to as the primary supply of fuel for strenuous physical activity. Carbohydrates are found almost exclusively in plant sources. Carbohydrates are classified as simple or complex. Examples of simple carbohydrates include table sugar, glucose, honey and molasses. Examples of complex carbohydrates include grains, beans, potatoes, vegetables and rice. Starches such as rice, potatoes, cereal grains and vegetables supply energy, vitamins, minerals, fiber and water. A healthy diet should be high in complex carbohydrates and low in simple carbohydrates. At least 50 to 60 percent of a health supporting diet should come from complex carbohydrates. It's important to remember that carbohydrates are not fattening. They supply only four calories per gram consumed, as compared to fats that offer nine calories per gram. Carbohydrates are only fattening when they are consumed with other fattening foods.

Protein

Proteins are often referred to as the building blocks of the body. Protein makes up approximately 18 to 20 percent of the human body. The main function of protein is for growth and repair. It is the structural basis for all body tissues. Protein can also be used for energy in some cases. The Recommended Daily Allowance (RDA) states that the daily protein requirement for active healthy adults is approximately 0.8 grams per kilogram of body weight. Certain individuals, such as growing athletes, people recovering from illness or athletes involved in strenuous resistance training programs, can consume up to 1.3 to 1.6 grams per kilogram of body weight per day. Consuming high quantities of protein will not lead to greater strength gains. A recent report by the National Research Council recommends that protein intake not exceed twice the RDA for anyone because of the convincing evidence that high protein intakes are associated with certain types of cancers and heart disease. Furthermore, a high protein intake places a heavy burden on the liver and kidneys to secrete excess nitrogen and may even damage those organs.

Protein sources include meat, fish, poultry, eggs, milk, cheese, nuts, dried peas, beans, bread, cereals and vegetables. Try to choose foods that are both high in protein and low in fat, such as fish, chicken, turkey, lean meats, low-fat cheese, skim milk and egg whites. Since the average individual living in the United States consumes twice the RDA for protein, there is no need to purchase expensive protein supplements.

Fats

Fat is a very concentrated source of energy. Fats contain twice as many calories (9) per gram as do carbohydrates (4 grams). Fat is a secondary source of energy and is the primary storage form of foods not immediately utilized by the body. Fat deposits in the body are a fuel reserve. According to the American Heart Association, no more than 30 percent of a diet should consist of fatty foods. A high percentage of fat intake can result in decreased efficiency of the body and place added stress on the heart and joints. Furthermore, a high fat diet leads to an increase in body fat, makes you feel tired and reduces athletic performance. Saturated fat sources include butter, cheese, chocolate, coconuts, oil, meats, milk and poultry. A good unsaturated fat source is oil.

Vitamins

Vitamins are non-caloric organic substances essential for building the body's cells, digestion, tissue building and energy release. Vitamins are present in small quantities in the body, and function to promote many chemical reactions that occur naturally in the body. The recommended daily allowances (RDA) have been established for most vitamins. There is absolutely no need to take large quantities of supplemental vitamins. In fact, this practice can be potentially dangerous. The preferred source of vitamins is a balance diet.

A Word On Antioxidant Vitamins

Over the past decade, there has been increasing scientific and public interest in the theoretical possibility that antioxidant vitamins, such as beta carotene (provitamin A), vitamin C and alpha-tocopherol (vitamin E) might prevent cancer and heart disease, and slow the aging process. Antioxidants help remove free radicals (highly reactive molecules with an unpaired electron) before they have a chance to cause cell damage. Observational epidemiologic data from both case-control and cohort studies have suggested that persons who take large amounts of antioxidant vitamins have somewhat lower than average risk of cancer and cardiovascular disease. Although the evidence is limited, consuming antioxidant vitamins might prevent some exercise-induced stress (lipid peroxidation, pentane and ethane excretion). Individuals should be cautious when reading exaggerated health claims for antioxidant vitamins. Further research is needed to clarify the benefits and potential risks of antioxidants. In the mean time, conservative recommendations have been published in the *University of California Berkley Wellness Letter* (1992).

People from all walks of life have been tempted at one time or another by the claims manufacturers make about vitamins. Unfortunately, if it sounds too good to be true, it probably is. There is a saying in sports that athletes have the most expensive urine around. Since the human body can only absorb a fixed amount of vitamins, at a fixed rate, most vitamins are washed out of the body in the urine. Most people would be far better off if they took the money they spent on vitamin supplements and bought more wholesome foods.

Minerals

Minerals are inorganic substances that exist freely in nature. Minerals are necessary for growth and repair of bones and teeth, metabolic activity, and function of body fluids and secretions. Minerals maintain or regulate such physiological processes as muscle contraction, normal heart rhythm and nerve impulse conduction. As with vitamins, mineral intake may also be abused. For people that are especially active and who sweat profusely for prolonged periods of time, it may be necessary to add additional salt and potassium to the diet. Both of these minerals can be easily replaced by drinking a commercially available sports drink, or by adding a little extra salt to the diet. Mineral sources include calcium (found in milk, cheese, egg yolk and green vegetables), iron (liver), iodine (seafood and iodized salt) and phosphorous (milk and cheeses).

Water

Approximately 70 percent of the total body weight is water. Water is the most important nutrient, involved in almost every vital body process. Water is essential for maintaining the body's temperature, transporting materials and assisting with chemical reactions. Two to three quarts of water should be ingested each day. Water levels in the body are maintained by drinking fluids, but also through the water contained in fruits and vegetables. With excess sweating, such as during exercise and in hot humid weather, a large amount of water is lost. In such cases, it is important to consume large quantities of water to remain hydrated.

Exercise sessions should be reduced or curtailed when the relative humidity exceeds 90 percent and/or when the air temperature exceeds 85°F. Children must be monitored carefully when exercising in the heat, since they are more susceptible to heat related illness than adults.

The intensity of the exercise should be gradually increased over a 10 to 14 day period when moving to a warmer environment.

Always be fully hydrated prior to exercising in any type of environment (hot or cold). Children may need to be forced to drink during exercise, since at least one study has shown that children will voluntarily dehydrate themselves during exercise.

These guidelines should be followed for ideal fluid replacement during exercise:

1. The fluid should contain no more than 10-20 mEq/L of sodium and no more than 6 to 8% glucose or sucrose.
2. The fluid should be cool (8 to 13°C).
3. Fluids should never be restricted during exercise.
4. For each pound of weight lost during exercise, 2 cups of fluid should be consumed before the next exercise session.
5. 2.5 cups of fluid should be consumed before exercise.
6. At least 1 cup of fluid should be consumed every 15 to 20 minutes during exercise.

In hot and humid environments, clothing should be lightweight in order to facilitate evaporation of sweat. In colder environments, layers of clothing provide an insulating barrier of air and can be changed as the ambient temperature increases or decreases.

Recommended Number of Servings Per Day

Bread Group — 11 servings
Vegetable Group — 5 servings
Fruit Group — 4 servings
Dairy Group — 2-3 servings
Meat Group — 3 servings

The Food Guide Pyramid

The Food Guide Pyramid is a new way to make the basics of a healthful diet easier to understand. It helps you make the right nutritional choices so that you can meet your nutrient needs. The Food Guide Pyramid allows you to select foods that together give you all the essential nutrients you need to maintain health, without eating too many calories or too much fat.

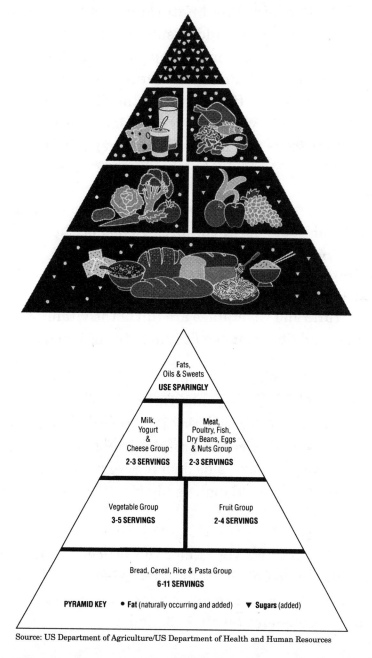

Source: US Department of Agriculture/US Department of Health and Human Resources

The Food Guide Pyramid consists of five basic food groups (levels 1-3) and the fats, oils and sweets commonly found in our diet (level 4). The size of the food group piece corresponds to the recommended number of daily servings from that food group. For example, the bread group piece is the largest in size and it has the greatest number of recommended servings.

The triangle and circle shapes scattered throughout the pyramid's pieces represent the added and naturally occurring fat and oil in certain foods, as well as the added sugars. Many triangles and/or circles in a food group piece mean that many of the foods in that category contain a large amount of naturally occurring or added fat and oil, and/or sugars. If you start at the bottom of the pyramid and work your way up, you will see how selections from the food groups and other foods can be pieced together to form a healthful overall diet.

Level 1 — Choose plenty of foods that come from plants. Bread, cereal, rice, and pasta form the broad base of the pyramid and should make up the bulk of your diet.

Level 2 — Also important is an ample variety of fruits and vegetables. Fruits and vegetables are full of the vitamins, minerals, carbohydrates and fiber you need to gain strength and stay healthy.

Level 3 — Add a moderate amount of lower-fat/lean foods from the milk group and the meat group. Dairy products provide calcium that's important for a healthy skeleton in everyone. Foods from the meat group provide needed protein, iron and zinc. When they are included in your diet as a side dish to accompany cereals, grains, fruits and vegetables, you'll make a big step toward strength gains and healthful eating.

Level 4 — Go easy on your selection of foods containing fats, oils and sweets. In moderation these foods can fit into an athletes diet. They should not, however, replace the nutrient-rich food choices found throughout levels 1, 2, and 3.

Examples of A Serving

Bread, Cereal, Rice, Pasta

1 slice of bread
1/2 bagel or hamburger bun
1 ounce of ready-to-eat cereal
1/2 cup of cooked cereal, rice or pasta

Vegetable

1 cup of raw leafy vegetables
1/2 cup of other vegetables, cooked or chopped raw 3/4 cup of
    vegetable juice

Fruits

1 medium apple, banana, orange
1/2 cup of chopped cooked or canned fruit
3/4 cup of fruit juice

Milk, Yogurt and Cheese

1 cup of milk or yogurt
1-1/2 ounce of natural cheese
2 ounces of processed cheese

Meat, Poultry, Fish, Dry Beans, Eggs, and Nuts

2-3 ounces of cooked lean meat, poultry, or fish
1/2 cup of cooked dry beans, 1 egg, or 2 tablespoons of peanut
    butter counts as 1 ounce of lean meat.

Remember To...

• Eat a variety of low fat foods from among all the five groups
(levels 1-3) each day. No one food or food group can provide
all the nutrients you need to develop a strong and healthy
body.

• Make plant foods such as cereal, grains, vegetables and fruit
the basis of your diet.

• Eat moderate amounts of low fat foods from the milk group and
the meat group.

• Go easy on fats, oils and sweets (those naturally occurring, as
well as those added).

Meals For Better Exercise Performance

The Pre-Exercise Meal

What you eat before you exercise will determine how well you
perform. A good pre-exercise meal helps to prevent hypoglycemia,
decrease hunger feelings during competition, provide energy for
the muscles and provide adequate fluids for the body. Instead of
the old standard athletic pregame meal of steak, eggs, toast and
potatoes, today's athletic pregame meal should includes foods
such as fruits, cooked vegetables, lean meats and bread. A pre-
exercise meal should be consumed no later than 2 1/2 hours before
exercise.

High Protein Diets

High protein diets and protein supplements have been popular
among weight trainers and body builders for years.
Unfortunately, athletes need no more protein than the average
individual. Furthermore, a well-balanced diet will supply
adequate amounts of protein. Protein supplementation is of no

value as far as performance is concerned. Muscle growth cannot be increased by eating excessive amounts of high-protein foods. Intake of high amounts of protein beyond an athlete's caloric requirement will only be stored as fat. Furthermore, high intakes of protein can lead to dehydration and loss of calcium in the body.

High Carbohydrate Meals

People who are athletic should consume meals that consist of high energy, low fat foods. Carbohydrates represent the most important fuel for muscular work. As your workouts increase in intensity, so should your carbohydrate intake. Carbohydrates are stored in the muscle as glycogen. When glycogen levels get depleted, fatigue sets in. When your muscles are sore and you feel fatigued, your glycogen stores have been depleted. Since glycogen is the principal carbohydrate used during exercise, athletes should eat a high carbohydrate meal before exercise to provide fuel for exercise and one after exercise to help replace the glycogen used up during exercise.

Sample High Energy, High Carbohydrate Menu

Breakfast

1 cup orange juice or 1/2 grapefruit
1 cup hot cereal
2 eggs
Bacon, ham, or sausage (3oz)
2-4 slices of whole wheat toast or hot cakes with margarine
Hot chocolate (1-2 cups)

Lunch

Bowl of clam chowder
Broiled fish (3-6 oz)
Cooked rice (1/2 cup)
Green salad with dressing
Bread (2 slices)
Milk (1-2 cups)

Dinner

Cream of potato soup
Broiled chicken (2 pieces)
Baked potato(es) (1-2)
Cooked broccoli (1-2 pieces)
Strawberries (3/4 cup)
Milk (1-2 cups)

Snacks

Fruits, especially dates, raisins, apples, bananas
More milk, or a milkshake
Cookies

CHAPTER 12

STAYING WITH IT

It has been estimated that 50% of people who start an exercise program quit within the first 6 months to one year. Not very good statistics, are they? Why do so many people drop out of exercise programs? This has been a highly investigated area for several years now. It doesn't matter how much you educate someone regarding the benefits of exercise, or motivate them to start an exercise program; if you can't get them to stay with it, it really doesn't matter what you have done. This chapter presents some helpful hints on how to stay with your exercise program.

Exercise Adherence Tips

Setting Goals

Setting realistic goals about your exercise program is one of the first things you can do to increase you exercise adherence rate. Ask yourself, why am I starting a walking program in the first place? Is it to lose weight, look better, improve my health, or lower my blood pressure? The reason(s) why you are starting an exercise program should be the primary guide to setting up your program. If your main reason to exercise is to lose weight, then you also need to plan your diet along with your exercise program. The safe recommendation for weight loss is 2 pounds per week. If you want to lose 2 pounds per week, you will need to cut back approximately 700 Kcal per day (700 x 7 = 4,900 Kcal/week) and exercise 5 days per week at an average caloric expenditure of 400 Kcal per day (2,000 Kcal). Since one pound of fat is equal to 3,500 Kcal, in order to lose two pounds per week you need to have a caloric deficit of nearly 7,000 calories per week. If this is your goal, you need to sit down and write out a plan.

An unrealistic goal would be to lose 20 pounds in one month. Even the goal of losing 2 pounds per week might be unrealistic for some people. Some people may not be willing to exercise that much or cut back on their calories that much. You need to decide what is right for you. Make sure you write down all of your goals. If you need to make any changes as time goes by, that's fine. What about setbacks? Say you end up gaining weight one week instead of losing any. Sit back and think what you may or may not have done to make this happen. Reassess your goals and see if you need to make any changes. The main point is that successful people set goals and stick to them. If you want to be a successful exerciser, set realistic goals and stick with them.

Location, Location, Location

One of the strongest factors associated with exercise adherence is how available your exercise location is. For example, if you join a health club that is on the other side of town just because they are running a special, you substantially increase your chances of not going to it, and thus not exercising. The nice thing about a walking program is that you can do it anywhere and anytime.

Fun

After I suffered a serious injury from running, I went to a variety of doctors and they all told me the same thing: Stop running and start swimming. Well, I hate to swim. No matter how much I tried to like it, I just never got the hang of it. So do you think swimming was a good suggestion for me? No, of course not. If you want to have a good chance at sticking with your exercise program, you have to choose an activity that you enjoy! I really have never met anyone who does not like to walk.

Rewards

A fun way to keep motivated with your exercise program is to reward yourself once and awhile. For example, after you lose 5 pounds you decide to buy yourself a new pair of shoes; after 10 pounds, a new outfit, etc. When you work hard for something, you deserve a reward.

Exercising With Others

Another important adherence factor is family or social support. You need to let your spouse, friends or co-workers know how important your exercise program is to you. Help them to help you succeed. Several studies have demonstrated that exercise adherence is increased when you exercise with another person or group of people. Exercising with a group of people provides reinforcement, camaraderie and support. Many people find it helpful to exercise with another individual. The "buddy system" has also shown to increase exercise adherence. If you set a time to exercise with someone, you are less likely to not show up because you will let the other person down.

Keep A Progress Chart

Keeping a workout log is a great way to monitor your progress or setbacks.

Cross Training

If you are staring to get depressed with your walking program, stop for awhile and do something else. Go for a bike ride or go swimming or just take a few days off.

Set A Time and Place To Exercise

Research has shown that if you set a specific time and place to exercise, you will be more likely to do it. Take a look at your schedule and try to determine what time is going to be best for you.

ENJOY!

Remember that you can really never fail at exercise. Any amount of exercise is good for you. Try to set realistic goals for your exercise program, and learn to enjoy it. If you need to get away from your exercise sessions once in awhile, then do it.

More than anything, just enjoy your exercise. Your walking sessions should be a time for yourself, a time to reflect and relax. I know many people, including myself, who use walking sessions to plan their day, solve problems, etc. Remember that exercise is a lifelong pursuit, so if you are going to do anything for that long, you'd better learn to enjoy it.